Dear ⸱

Open Heaven!!!

Betty Charles

Journals of
VICTORY

Vision for My Life

BETTY CHARLES

 FriesenPress

One Printers Way
Altona, MB R0G 0B0
Canada

www.friesenpress.com

ISBN
978-1-03-915316-5 (Hardcover)
978-1-03-915315-8 (Paperback)
978-1-03-915317-2 (eBook)

1. BIOGRAPHY & AUTOBIOGRAPHY, RELIGIOUS

Distributed to the trade by The Ingram Book Company

This book is dedicated for you.

Are you one of those who were given a vision, task, or a dream to do but you said "I can't", because you don't know where to start or how to do, and don't believe you can do it?

You may be one who thinks "It's too 'big', no way I can do it. This is impossible!"

Or maybe you are just making excuses that you don't want to do it.

Or maybe you are still waiting for your God given vision. Not to worry! God will if you seek Him in His perfect time.

I have good news for you! You are not alone. I have been in those shoes before. Know that if it's God's will, He will help you through. Obedience and commitment to God is the key to success.

With God, there is nothing impossible! With God, you are able! Trust him!

God's servant,
Betty Charles

Introduction

We are not going to sweep our God given dreams, vision and talents under the carpet nor forget about it. We need not fear or make excuses. We just need to understand the truth. The Bible declares:

"Before I formed you in the womb I knew you, and
before you were born, I consecrated you, I have
appointed you a prophet to the nations."
Jeremiah 1:5

This powerful scripture tells us that all of us have a purpose, plan, and a destiny designed by God before we were born.

"It is our responsibility to find it! But, seek His
kingdom and His righteousness, and all
these things will be added to you."
Matthew 6:33

As you read the revelation shared in this book on how I reached my given God vision to victory, remember that you are reading for a definite reason; it's a divine appointment. Even if you didn't intend to buy this book but picked it up randomly or a friend gave it to you, the Holy Spirit has a definite purpose for your life. Nothing in life happens by chance. God has no accidents!

"Therefore, I say to you, "all things for which you pray
and ask, believe that you have received them,
and they will be granted to you."
Mark 11:24

Just about everything that we receive from our Heavenly Father, both in the natural and spiritual world, is based upon our dreams and desires.

We must desire victorious Christian living or it will never be ours.

When we are living a defeated, compromising, and powerless Christian life, we have to honestly desire the better life that Christ can give or it will never come.

When we have unsaved loved ones, we must desire and intercede for their salvation from the depths of our beings before spiritual forces are set in motion that will change the course of their lives, their thinking, and their spiritual insight to bring them to Christ.

The same is true regarding our dream come true. When we have a dream, vision, and a desire in our heart, we must have the desire to reach and fulfill the dream and vision or else divine supernatural forces will not be put into action on our behalf. NEVER QUIT!

Wishful thinking is not enough. You must act upon our desire and vision. The Bible declares:

"The effectual (fervent) prayer of a righteous
man can accomplish much."
James 5:16

Prayer is a mighty weapon at the disposal of every man and woman who loves God, and knows His son Jesus Christ. It also energizes the heart of a believer through the power of the Spirit. Consistent prayer also releases the power of God's blessing on our lives and circumstances.

Remember this, God wants us to have complete victory in our lives. He wants us whole in body, mind, and spirit. Many people believe that something they are going through, which is causing them affliction, is God's will and that they can't live in the power of the Holy Spirit and experience victory.

This is not simply true! God sent His only begotten Son into the world so that He might destroy the work of the devil.

"For this purpose, the Son of God was manifested that
he might destroy the works of the devil."
1 John 3:8

Jesus died so that we might have victory in our bodies, minds, souls, and spirits. Don't let the devil tell us that we can't. God wants to use us as vessels. God wants us victorious.

This book will tell you about the vision God gave me 18 years ago. God said *"build me a church"* when I was at the first Evangelical conference I attended in California, just three months after I received Jesus as my personal Savior. I was not sure on what this meant. I was not sure how to go about it. I had so many questions, the five "Ws" and "H". It was scary and unbelievable that God chose me. Fear came upon me. Who am I that God chose me?

"Just as He chose us in Him before the
foundation of the world, that we would be holy
and blameless before Him in love."
Ephesian 1:4

Why was I afraid? It was fear of failure, fear of being the object of ridicule, fear of being a minority, fear that what God said was not true. Fear has been stated to be man's worst enemy, and this has been repeatedly proven to be true. President Franklin Delano Roosevelt said, "The only thing we have to fear is fear itself." Where does fear come from? The Bible says:

> *"There is no fear in love; but perfect love cast out fear: because fear involves punishment, and the one who fears is not perfected in love. We know that this type of fear does not come from God."*
> *1 John 4:18*

Paul said to Timothy;

> *"For God has not given us a fear of timidity, but of power and love and discipline."*
> *2 Timothy 1:7*

If this fear does not come from God, it must have come from Satan.

In every truth, there is the negative and a positive side. Did you know there is a positive side of fear? Most believers think of fear as our enemy, but fear can also be a blessing in disguise. If fear drives us to our knees to travail with a fervency which moves the hand of God that moves the world, then that fear has been a positive influence in our life. It has forced us into closer relationships and communions with God, and therefore has worked for our good. If fear drove us to the Word of God to have us seek answers from Him, then fear has accomplished a great work in our lives. Sad to say, in many cases, fear is the only thing that will accomplish these objectives in our lives.

*"Jehoshaphat was afraid and turned his attention
to seek the Lord and proclaimed a fast
throughout all Judah."*
2 Chronicles 20:3

The scripture declares, Jehoshaphat was afraid, and when he was afraid, he set himself to seek the face of God. Fear acted as a spur to stir him to seek the Lord.

Most people reading this book will fall into two categories:

- **One:** Do you have a vision, dream, or a desire in your heart that you are afraid to go forward and pursue?

- **Two:** Are you seeking the Lord to give you your purpose and destiny and question what your calling in your life is? Do you want God to use you? What is your Ministry?

I consider myself under category One. I was given a vision but I was afraid to go forward and pursue the vision. Year after year passed by as I was praying, seeking, asking and knocking to God, and after 18 years, He finally fulfills my dream. Praise God! HOW? I will tell you my journey to the Promised Land. It's a long journey but it's worth waiting. You can do it too!

That is the reason why I wrote this book.

SECTION 1

Vision

It all started when I received Jesus in my heart as my personal Savior. Last December 3, 2003, I reluctantly participated in an Encounter Weekend up North of Ontario, Canada, led by Pastor Sue. I was with my daughters Rayma and Rowena, and a full bus load of men and women of Christ. I just went because my two daughters wanted me to experience God's supernatural power and His presence. I was not sure what to expect but I went with a closed mind. I was basically forced to go.

Before the Encounter, we had 12 weeks of Pre-encounter classes which I did not enjoy and did not participate, due to the fact that I have already converted once, from Catholic to Anglican, when I got married to my husband, Michael. My daughters wanted me to convert to "Born Again." I could not bear the idea to get converted to another religion again. When the pastor who was teaching the first night said "Unless you are born again, you cannot enter the kingdom of God", that did it for me. I did not want to go to another session for 11 weeks, but my daughter, Rowena, begged me to accompany her and I did persevere for her sake.

After 12 weeks of classes, the time to go to Encounter Weekend came. We rode in a school bus heading up to North of Toronto. The trip was uneventful.

We arrived there late Friday night. The instruction given to us was not to talk to anyone. We are supposed to be still and be quiet all night. Early Saturday morning, we got up and went for breakfast. After breakfast, we gathered in the foyer and we all were given a rusty nail and about 7 to 8 pages of papers with all the sins (from little lies to murder, name it) were all listed.

I was just a new kid in the block so I tried to follow instructions. It all started with the "physical touch" activity where we used the rusty nail. We were supposed to reflect on what Jesus did in Calvary at the cross. Then, we were asked to look at all the list of sins we might have done, mark them and hold on to them for the rest of the day. Later that night, we gathered again at the foyer, confessed and repented all the sins we marked in the papers. One by one, we put the sheets of paper into the fireplace and sent them to heaven. The way I confessed and repented was pretty amazing, but my heart was not yet open. I was still resistant to receive any messages that was given that day. My ears, eyes, and mind were still closed shut.

The following day, I tried my best to be more open minded and hear what this encounter is all about. We had services and preachers in the morning, but my heart was not ready and still resistant to go respond to altar call.

In the afternoon service, there was a young girl named Paty, 13 years old, who was preaching. Her message was so powerful that I was receiving it from her as if God was talking to me. I had my eyes closed all the time and it is as if I heard God talking to me.

In that moment, everything changed. I was touched by her preaching and that I stood up to go to the altar. I was shaking, crying, tears falling down my cheeks and I was even laughing. The attendees were all laughing and crying together with joy, jumping, and just feeling freedom. It was a great experience. I gave my heart to Jesus wholeheartedly. It was at that moment when I felt the touch of God. I was crying of joy and peace, and I felt all my burdens were lifted. I was shaking, laughing, crying, and shouting for joy. I felt so renewed and felt like a brand-new creation. In that moment, I received my freedom and my life changed. Amen!

I AM SAVED! I AM NOT AFRAID!
I AM FREE TO SAVE THE LOST!

January 10, 2004
It was shocking to find out that Rayma was diagnosed with Stage 4 Breast Cancer while she was pregnant and was due for delivery on January 14, 2004. She was only 34 years old with two precious boys, Tyler and Austin. Rayma's faith was very strong. She loved ministering to others, and loved homeless people. She had a very good heart for the needy. I remember the time when she was about to deliver Austin, her second son; I was driving her to the Hospital when she saw a homeless man on the street and she wanted me to stop so she can give him some money. Then, she was checked by the doctor and said she is not due for a few more hours, so she asked me to take her to have her nails done, and she felt good.

It was one of my proudest days when a baby girl arrived last January 14, 2004. Her name is Zoe which means "new life." She is a miracle baby and a beautiful one. She was born with a cleft palate, so she had to be fed with a special nipple and she had high risk of getting aspirated.

While she was only a month old, I was holding her and feeding her as usual when she suddenly stopped breathing and turned blue. My husband called the ambulance and in the meantime, with my experience as a nurse, I was able to revive her. By the time the ambulance arrived, she was okay. Praise God!

In March of 2004, I went to an Evangelical Conference in California. I was so hungry to get to know Jesus. I wanted to learn what to do and see how Christians' worship and meet people who are close to God, and most importantly, to receive what God had for me. Also, I went hoping for my daughter Rayma to be healed from Cancer. It was such a difficult journey, that I turned to God, seeking God for my daughter's healing. My main goal is to go and ask prayers to heal Rayma, but God gave me a different task: I ran to the altar call and I was at the front of the stage. The people were just pouring in front and as the Prophet reached the stage and started preaching, I had my eyes closed, I saw some stars and I heard the voice of God saying, "build me a church."

I was stunned, afraid of what that meant. That night I was asking God the "5 W's and an H". Who? What? When? Where? Why? and How? I was overwhelmed!

After the conference, I came home and told Rayma and my family what happened, Rayma who had been a Christian for a few years and been reading the Bible cover to cover, day and night, said: "Mom you need to pray about it, it is from God." And this gave me more fear of the unknown; where is this church going to be built, when is this going to happen, why me? Who is going to help me, and how am I going to afford to build this church? Whew! Too much, too big of a vision!

I often wonder if this is even possible. So, while searching for an answer of all my questions, while reading the newspaper one day, I come across an article about a church for sale in Niagara Falls. We went to see the building and inquire about the details but did not fan out.

"Before I formed you in the womb, I knew you before
you were born, I set you apart. I appointed you
as a prophet to the nations."
Jeremiah 1:5

This Scripture gave me strength and courage to wait for the Lord. I believed that if this is from God, it will be done on his perfect time.

SECTION 2

Seeking: Why Me?

Who am I?

> *"Who are chosen according to the foreknowledge of*
> *God the Father, by the sanctifying work of the Spirit,*
> *to obey Jesus Christ and be sprinkled with His blood:*
> *May peace be yours in the fullest measures."*
> *1Peter 1:1-2*

Wow, what a revelation! What a privilege to hear from God that He chose me and He knew me before I was born, by the sanctifying work of the Spirit and I was sprinkled with His blood. All I needed to do was OBEY Jesus Christ. He was giving me peace and grace in the fullest measure.

The definition of seeking is an attempt or desire to obtain or achieve something. Here I am, seeking God to continuously guide and direct my path to fulfill his promise to me.

I am seeking God's good guidance and not evil.

"Seek good and not evil, that you may live;
and thus, may the Lord God of Host be
with you, just as you have said."
Amos 5:14

"But seek first His Kingdom and His righteousness
and all the things will be added to you."
Matthew 6:33

"Ask and it will be given to you, seek and you will find,
knock and it will be opened to you."
Matthew 7:7

"Therefore, if you have been raised up with Christ,
keep seeking the things above, where Christ is,
seated at the right hand of God."
Colossians 3:1

"I love those who love me and those who
diligently seek me will find me."
Proverbs 8:17

SECTION 3

Praying

THE LORD'S PRAYER

Our Father who is in heaven
Hallowed be your name
Your kingdom come
Your will be done
On earth as it is in heaven.
Give us this day our daily bread.
And forgive us our debts, as we also have forgiven our debtors.
And do not lead us into temptation, but deliver us from evil.
For yours is the kingdom and the power
and the glory forever. Amen.

This is my constant prayer every day, praising Him for who He is. His name is above all name.

Jehovah Jireh my provider, Jehovah Shalom my
Prince of Peace, My Lord of lords, King of kings.
The Great I am, The Alpha and Omega, the beginning
and the end. My good Shepherd, who protects me, feed
me, lead me and guide me. My Jehovah Shammah,
always with me, He is everywhere.
Let your will be done! Let your Kingdom come!
Lead me not into temptation and deliver me from evil.
God forgive my trespasses as I forgive others.
For thine is the kingdom the power and the
glory forever Amen.

"Meditate on the word day and night."
Joshua 1:8

This verse talks about meditating or thinking deeply and focusing our mind on the Word of God. In it, God commands Joshua to meditate on His Word, day and night, to become prosperous and successful.

With a lot of seeking and praying, God opened a big door for me. My Uncle Erning, from California, called me and asked me to be one of their bridesmaids for their 50th wedding anniversary in September 2007.

Wow! What a surprise! I have not gone back to the Philippines since I came to Canada in April 3, 1967. Forty years is a long time. It was a privilege to be able to go alone, with my husband and children's blessings and support.

While in the Philippines, we went to visit my village, Abour. God showed me that this was the location and place where the church is to be built. I saw that the people definitely needed Jesus. There was no progress at all since I left, and the people there were all with the same lifestyle. There was no change after 40 years. There were so much hardships, frustrations, brokenness, poverty, and family circumstances in this town. They needed Jesus to change their reputation and circumstances. I was convicted to lead these people in my hometown to salvation. They are lost!

"The next day, He purposed to go to Galilea, and He found Philip, and Jesus said to Him, 'Follow Me'. Nathaniel said to Him, 'Can any good thing come out of Nazareth?' Philip said, 'Come and see.' Jesus saw Nathaniel coming to Him and said to him, 'Behold, an Israelite indeed, in whom there is no deceit!' Nathaniel said to Him, 'How do you know me?' Jesus answered and said to him, 'Before Philip called you, when you were under the fig tree, I saw you.' Nathaniel answered Him, 'Rabbi, you are the Son of God; You are the King of Israel.' Jesus answered and said to him, 'Because I said to you that I saw you under the fig tree, do you believe? You will see greater things than these.' And He said to him, 'Truly, truly, I say to you, you will see the heavens opened and the angels of God ascending and descending on the Son of Man.'"
John 1:43-51

It is documented in history that Nazareth, one of the lowliest places on earth, is a place where nothing good could come out of it. No wonder then that Nathaniel rehashed this historical truth to his friend, Philip.

Nathaniel looked at his naked eye about Nazareth- a messed up place, lots of hardship, frustration with life circumstances. He sees nothing is working.

What is your Nazareth? My Nazareth is for the people in my village, Abour, to give their heart to Jesus and have a relationship with Jesus, because Jesus can change the reputation of his people, not only in my village, but for "ALL" his people.

These answers my "WHY'S."

I believe that this is the key to my victory. Prayer and diligent meditation are so important to God. Daily communion with Him as soon I wake up is what God wants. He wants to be first; he is a jealous God. Don't put Him last or don't forget to talk to Him. He is always available to talk to us. He is never too busy for us. He does not need us. We need Him. Don't just pray when we need something.

Praise Him!

SECTION 4

First Mission
(Banaue, Ifugao) Philippines

"Making known to us the mystery, the secret of His
will, His plan, of His purpose; and it is this in accor-
dance with the good pleasure, His merciful intention
which He hath previously purposed and set forth in
Him. He planned for the maturity of the times
and the climax of the ages."
Ephesians 1:9-10

I say, that the God I serve is a God of plan, purpose, design and objectivity.

"And he said to them, 'Go into all the world and
preach the gospel to all creation.'"
Mark 16:15

Bethel Gospel Tabernacle in Hamilton were asking for Missionary volunteers to Banaue, Philippines last March 2008. There were five of us; Pastor Randy, his wife Esther, Martha a retired teacher and Lisa a mother, and myself a Retired nurse for 46 years of service.

Then, I embarked on my first Mission trip. I have not gone to a Mission trip before, so I don't know what to do and what am I expected to do. I went for experience. When I was working as a Travel nurse and advising missionaries to go to different countries, I had a desire to experience going to a mission one day, and that was my chance that God gave me.

The reason Jesus commissioned us with these great tasks, knowing our human nature despite the weaknesses and our failures, was because when He looked at us, He was not looking at what we were. He was looking at what He could make of us.

We arrived at Noah's Ark orphanage house, located in Banaue, Ifugao, Philippines. It's a place of temporary home for orphans, abandoned, special needs, malnourished, and educationally disadvantaged children. There were 10 babies and toddlers, 22 elementary and high school students, 6 college students, and 16 special needs children. The high school students came from single-parent raised families and live in very far-flung villages. In the home, they receive proper nutrition, education and love. The special needs children mostly suffer from cerebral palsy with different degrees. Through this ministry, the children were given a chance for a brighter future and to have an opportunity to come into a relationship with God.

Up to date, more than 250 children lived in the Home and more than 750 children received educational and emergency assistance, all thanks to the work and dedication of the person who started the orphanage, Linda, who is also from Canada. I admire her dedication, her hard work and enthusiasm to care for these children.

During our two-week stay, we accomplished a Vacation Bible Study for children aged 5 years to 11 years of age. This went on for a week. The week after, we executed the same for the 12 years of age and older ones which went on for five days. We made crafts, played games, and read Bible verses. Every day, we had about 125 children line up by the gate before the opening; children that were so happy and excited to come and learn about God. They learned memory verses every day and they were very good at it.

It was a very tiring and exhausting experience, but it was worth it. Having the chance to be around these young enthusiastic children made me feel young again.

During our trip, I was also worried about my daughter, Rayma, who was fighting for her life against Cancer. She was diagnosed in 2004 but her body started to deteriorate in 2007. She was in and out of the Hospital, but in January 2008 she was transferred to Bob Kemp Hospice with the anticipation that she did not have much time to live. I tried to cancel my trip but Rayma insisted that I should go. She said, "Mom don't worry about me, I want you to go. I will be okay." That was the reason I went. I believed I did my duty for the Lord.

SECTION 5

Finding a Location

I was faced with another challenge in my life: finding a location for the church. This was another reason why I came to this mission trip. After the group left, I stayed for another week because I wanted to find a property for the church. On my first day, my cousin, Carrie, took me to my village, Abour, and found a property perfect for the church's building. It belonged to my maternal grandmother's sister, late Lola Osiang Florendo Ramirez. I made a deal with one of her sons and the property was secured and paid for. Praise God!

It was shocking for me that everything I needed was just at the tip of my fingers. I believed that God went before me, did all the work, and when I got there, everything was done. The next day, I got a surveyor to study the lot and an Engineer to do a Perspective Architectural plan. God did it all for me! Thank God!

By that time, I was confident that God is always with me in my journey and that His Word is true. All I needed to do was to listen and obey His command and His will.

It was my joy to see Rayma alive and to see the rest of my family. Thank God! It was also a joy to let Rayma know that we had the property secured for the church. Rayma was so happy to hear that we found the property for the church which she believed that God has commanded me to do.

That time, the WHERE question had been answered. THANK YOU, JESUS!

It was my saddest moment when Rayma passed away last July 29, 2008. She was only 39 years old. She left us with three beautiful grandchildren; Tyler, Austin and Zoe. What a blessing! She was no longer suffering. I believe that she is with the Lord, an angel watching over us. We will soon see her again in heaven.

SECTION 6

Finances

I have secured a property for the church, what's next? "WHERE" will the money come from? Thankfully, we had the funds to buy the property outright. I needed more prayers and breakthrough, since I acquired this ruined building that is not fit to live in. Squatters were living in it.

Way back 2008, the engineer told me that it would cost about two hundred fifty thousand dollars to build the Architectural Perspective. I wonder what would it be now, especially after Pandemic.

With more seeking, more prayers and meditation, and reading His Word daily, one day God told me to "restore the existing structure."

October 2010

Then, I asked Uncle Erning to contact a contractor whom he knows and requested to get me an estimate on how much did it cost to fix the place. Then, I got a quote of about thirteen thousand dollars for a good restoration. It included a new post, new bricks, new floor, new roof, two Comfort rooms, one for male and one for female.

When I looked at my savings account for the church, I had just enough money to have the work done. The money were my pay checks from Usana that I get every month for selling Vitamins. My family, including Rayma, used Usana vitamins which I still use up to now. I believe on premium high-quality vitamins.

SECTION 7

Building Restoration

With great planning and seeking God's guidance, on January 18, 2011, I went back to the Philippines to have the repairs done. At this point, I didn't have a specific plan. I was just trusting God that I will find a Pastor to do the service and be a shepherd for the lost sheep. I stayed in my uncle's place in Tinaan, Sta Maria. I arrived on January 18, 2011. I started inquiring about a pastor to lead Rayma Worship Center. A lady called a pastor that she knew and he agreed to come and meet me on January 19 in the afternoon. He came with his wife. There was a birthday cake in the house because it happened to be my birthday.

Surprisingly, the pastor said that it was also his birthday. Not only that, his wife's name is also Betty. Was this a divine appointment or what? Was this God's plan? I believed that God went before me and set His plan for me. He pre-arranged and provided all that I needed for this trip.

We talked and he agreed to be the lead Pastor for Rayma Worship Center. We went to look at the site with his wife and said that they will work together. So, the construction began as scheduled. Praise God!

I bought 100 chairs and some musical instruments for the church as well.

Knowing that the job will not be done before I leave to come home, I scheduled a dedication service to take place on February 15, 2011.

The night before the dedication service, I asked God, "Why did He chose to build the church at the middle of the Abour village?" I also said, "I remember, I grew up with my paternal grandfather as a child in the northern part of the village and my parents built a house in the south side of the village. But 'why' did you have me build a church at the middle of the village?" God said, "My child you were born behind that building. I am bringing you back where your life began." Whaaaaat?

I could not sleep that night. In the morning, I told Uncle Erning, who is the youngest brother of my dad, about the revelation of God. Uncle confirmed to me that it was true. I was born during World War II and my parents were hiding me and my older brother in a little nipa house just behind the church building. The Japanese were killing young children with their swords. What a revelation! I found it mysterious! This showed that God saved me from the Japanese soldiers because He had a plan and a purpose for my life.

While writing the book, this reminded me of the war in Ukraine and Russia. I saw how the families were scattered all over the place, trying to find a safe place for their children and families. It gave me the chills, while remembering how my parents managed to keep us safe from the Spaniards. I can imagine how the people in Ukraine are dealing with uncertainty and fear for the lives of their children and families. I am praying for Ukraine and their people that God will protect and provide for them, and lead them to a safe place also. This will be a great testimony for all the people that survived, like me.

During my devotion, a verse came to me;

> *"I have certainly seen the oppression of my people in*
> *Egypt and have heard their groans, and I have come*
> *now, and I will send you to Egypt."*
> *Acts 7:34*

Do you know that God speaks to us when we spend time with Him in prayer, meditation, and praises?

If you are not sure about the gift, calling and purpose of God for your life, try setting a specific time appointment with God daily. You will be amazed!

Praise God! I thank God for His provision. He provided all that I needed for this trip. Mission accomplished again. I was not responsible for all these accomplishments. It was all God's doing! I was just following His direction and command. He provides! He protects! He directs! And He does everything to finish the task He will give you.

I also thank God for my late daughter, Rayma, who led me to Christ my Savior. She saved me, rescued me, and redeemed me. Without her, all these Divine appointments and experiences would not happen.

My life changed since I met Him and knew that I have an intimate relationship with Him. He is faithful! He is always with me in the good and bad times. His love never fails. He is omnipotent and omnipresent. My life is dependent on Him. I could not do things without Him.

SECTION 8

Finding the Right Shepherd

Unfortunately, the first pastor did not last. He was not doing Sunday service and just left and abandoned the place without notice.

I found another pastor through someone from Canada. I contacted him and he also agreed to lead Rayma Worship Center. I was sending money monthly but I found out that there was no service or work done in the church. Again, he abandoned the place and left without notice.

I found it very frustrating to have had no one I can trust when I live far away. Again, I sought God's help and guidance to find a pastor who's trustworthy, a hard worker and dedicated to serve the Lord. I need MORE FERVENT PRAYERS!

At this point, I was again searching and seeking God's direction for another Pastor to use the church without charge, with the condition they maintain and keep the church clean and in good repair. I decided not to send more money, and in return, they can keep the tithing and offering which I did not benefit from previous pastors also.

In September 2016, I happened to call my cousin's wife, Loling, and she told me that she knew a Pastor who was doing Bible Study in someone's backyard. I asked her to find out his number so I can connect with him. Then, we spoke and he told me that they have been praying for a church in Abour for a long time. He told me to speak to his Senior Pastor. I spoke to his Senior Pastor and he was so happy and thankful for the offer. He asked me to write a letter to give him authority to manage the property. He then assigned a Pastor to do service every Sunday and conduct a once-a-week Bible Study. He kept all the offerings and they were the ones who paid the electric bills. Again, there was no communication or report from him. I assumed everything is good.

During this time, there was this burning desire for me to go to another Mission Trip.

I prayed to God again to open doors for me to serve the Lord. I remember attending a ladies' conference at Bethel Gospel Tabernacle in Hamilton. The story is about Martha and Mary.

> "Now as they were travelling along, He entered a
> village; and a woman named Martha welcomed Him
> into her home. So, she had a sister called Mary, who
> was seated at the Lord's feet, listening to His Word. But
> Martha was distracted with all the preparation; and
> she came up to Him and said, do you not care that my
> sister has left me to do all the serving alone? Then tell
> her to help me." But the Lord answered and said to
> her," Martha, Martha, you are worried and bothered
> about so many things; but only one thing is necessary,
> for Mary has chosen the good part, which shall not be
> taken away from her."
> Luke 10:38-42

The aforementioned passage is a tale of two sisters. One got caught up in chores. One got caught up with her Lord. The difference between Martha and Mary was that:

Martha was distracted by serving Jesus.

It doesn't mean that Martha was bad. She wasn't doing anything wrong in this story. She was serving God in a different way than Mary. She invited Jesus, her Savior, into her home and wanted Him to have a restful experience, and Martha became frustrated when her sister Mary didn't help her.

Mary took time out of her busy day, stopped what she was doing, and sat at her Savior's feet to listen to His teachings, even when it wasn't accepted by others. Mary knew that Jesus, the King of kings, was at her house, and she wasn't going to waste this opportunity. And according to Jesus, "Mary has chosen the good portion, which will not be taken away from her."

Mary's personal relationship with Jesus wasn't going to be taken away by anyone or anything - not by distractions of service or for eternity.

It's a matter of good versus best!

My question for you and me:

Will you choose what's best over good?

Personally, I have chosen to be Mary at my age of 77. I was Martha all my life. I helped all my family come to Canada. I helped most of the family of my in-laws came to Canada as well. I was always helping people in need, from little things to big things. Being a retired nurse, a caregiver to my sick daughter and husband, and raising children and grandchildren, I think I am done with my Martha role. It's time for me to serve the Lord to make up for what I did not do when I was younger. God has forgiven me.

From that conference day onwards, I changed and started to focus more on what the Lord wanted me to do. Building a church was a big responsibility and it came with lots of hurdle to be faced.

But with God's help and guidance, I knew that the day would come when it will be completed. Praying!

"As for me and my house, we will serve the Lord."
Joshua 14:15

SECTION 9

Mission #2

Last July 15, 2017, I sold our two-story house at Bonaparte Way, Hamilton. We have lived there for 20 years and I moved to our cottage by the lake at Bluewater Parkway in Selkirk which we owned for over 35 years. What a blessing it was! We wanted to sell it for quite some time but somehow, it was not sold. Moreover, our late daughter, Rayma, told us to never sell it. Again, I thank her, she was right. I believe that it was all in God's plan.

October 2017 came, I was searching for a church in my area and I happened to go to Kingsway Church. I met a nice couple asking me what country I am from. I answered that I was from the Philippines. Their eyes lit up and couldn't resist telling me that they are going to the Philippines to a Mission Trip sponsored by Sweets Church, a sister church of Kingsway. I told them that I have been praying and wanting to go on a Mission Trip. I got in touch with Wes Devries and was accepted to join the group. The Trip was scheduled for Feb, 18, 2018 in Cagayan de Oro. This group has been going to the Philippines over the past 20 years. They are very much involved in sending Sea Containers almost every year and they take a group of volunteers with them.

The Mission work they do is amazing. I learned a lot from this trip. Even with my disability from Rheumatoid Arthritis, I was able to hop in a Jeepney, went to the mountains to distribute goods to the poor. We saw the people so happy and excited from little things that were given to them. We also did a feeding program in a Tribe up in the Mountain. The dried vegetables from Canada were served to people. Children and adults lined up and were so excited to have a bowl of soup. They provided their own bowl or container. We also did a Street Ministry where they supplied a truck with all the instrumental equipment. People would stop and listen to the message, wanted to talk and asked questions about Jesus.

People received Christ in a mall. Some were taxi drivers, restaurants staff, and hotel staff. There were numerous miracles! It was an amazing experience. I loved it. I think I am addicted!

It is a good addiction for me.

I stayed two weeks behind and went to visit Rayma Worship Center. It was shocking and upsetting to see the condition of the Lord's house. It was so bad that the ceiling was moldy and leaking, and the electrical wiring was disconnected. The two washrooms were a mess. They were very dirty and disgusting. The bathroom doors were broken. The building was in state of disarray, the house of the Lord was not suitable for a place of worship. My heart was broken and hurt to see the way the church was. There was not even a sign outside the church to indicate that it is a worship center. I left some money to the Senior Pastor to have a signage made outside the church but he never got it done. I also sent one thousand dollars to his wife's name to do some repairs.

During my stay, I met Madam X who is from America. She lives in America during the summer and goes to the Philippines during the winter. She has a beautiful house in Santa, which is about 45 minutes away from the church.

SECTION 10

Mission #3
Repairs, Struggles
and Bumps

After my mission trip in 2017, God gave me another vision: to organize a Mission Trip to go repair the damages at Rayma Worship Center. This was birthed in January 26, 2019. It took a year of preparation and planning, and recruiting people who are interested to join the Mission. There were eight people interested to join; Mark, a farmer and handyman, a retired nurse, a flight attendant, Lily who is a dog breeder, a retired steel worker, a truck driver, and a pastor from CDO to help us organize a mini crusade, Daniela who is a 17 years old High school student, and Zoe who is 16 years old and is my granddaughter. Every one of them is given a special talent from God.

"For it is just like a man about to go on a journey, who called his own slaves and entrusted his possessions to them. To one he gave five talents, to another, two, and to another, one, each according to his own ability; and he went on his journey. Immediately, the one who had received the five talents went and traded with them, and gained five more talents. In the same manner, the one who had received the two talents gained two more. But he who received one talent went away, and dug a hole in the ground and hid his master's money. Now after a long time the master of those slaves came and settled accounts with them. The one who had received the five talents came up and brought five more talents, saying, 'Master, you entrusted five talents to me. See, I have gained five more talents.' His master said to him, 'Well done, good and faithful slave. You were faithful with a few things; enter into the joy of your master.' Also, the one who had received the two talents came up and said, 'Master, you entrusted two talents to me. See, I have gained two more talents.' His master said to him, 'Well done, good and faithful slave. You were faithful with the few things; I will put you in charge of many things; enter into the joy of your master.' And the one also who had received the one talent came up and said, 'Master, I knew you to be a hard man, reaping where you did not sow and gathering where you scattered no seed. And I was afraid and went away and hid your talent in the ground. See, you have what is yours.' But his master answered and said to him, 'You wicked, lazy slave, you knew that I reap where I did not sow and gather where I scattered no seed. Then you ought to have put my money in the bank, and on my arrival, I would have received my money back with *interest. Therefore, take away the talent from him, and give it to the one who has the ten talents.' For to everyone who has, more shall be given, and he will have abundance, but the one who does not have, even what he does have shall be taken away. Throw out the worthless slave into the outer darkness; in that place there will be weeping and gnashing of teeth. But when the Son of Man comes in His glory, and all the angels with Him, then He will sit on His glorious throne. All the nations will be gathered before Him; and He will separate them from one another, as the shepherd separates the sheep from the goats; and He will put the sheep on His right, and the goats on the left. Then the King will say to those on His right, 'Come, ye who are blessed of My Father, inherit the kingdom prepared for you from the foundation of the world. For I was hungry, and you gave Me something to eat; I was thirsty, and you gave Me something to drink; I was stranger, and you invited Me in; naked, and you clothe Me; I was sick, and you visited Me; I was in prison, and you came to Me.' Then the righteous will answer Him, 'Lord, when did we see you hungry and feed You, and give something to drink; And when did we see You a stranger; and invite You in, or naked and clothe You? When did we see You sick, or in prison, and come to You?' The King will answer and see to them, 'Truly I say to you, even the least of them you did it to Me.' Then He will also say to those on His left, 'Depart from Me, accursed ones, into the eternal fire which has been prepared for the devil and his angels; for I was hungry and you gave Me nothing to eat; I was thirsty and you gave Me nothing to drink; I was a stranger, and you*

did not invite Me in; naked, and you did not clothe
Me; and in prison, and you did not visit Me.' Then
they themselves also will answer, 'Lord, when did we
see you hungry, and did not care of You? Then He will
answer them, Truly I say to you, to the extent that you
did not do it to one of the least of these, you did not do
it to Me.' These will go away into eternity punishment,
but the righteous into the eternal life.'"
Matthew 24:14-26

These eight various aged men and women had talents. In this parable, the "talent" represents not only money but the individual gifts, skills, time, energy, education, intellects, strength, influential and opportunities. Every one of them have a unique personality and character.

Be very careful when choosing people to come to a Mission, with or without experience. Find someone who is focused on serving the Lord and able to adjust to whatever needs to be done for the Lord. Mission trips are not considered a vacation or a relaxation. It involves hard work, creativity, and focus on the needs of the people around you and the community.

If you are desiring to join a mission group, make sure that you seek God's guidance to mold you, equip you and use you for His glory.

We talked and learned about **A Life of Faithfulness** before going into the mission field.

How can we be faithful (verse 21-23)

USE IT OR LOSE IT
Be faithful with whatever you have been given. It is no good wishing that you had been given more. You are simply called to do the best you can with what you have.

To be faithful means to use the gifts and abilities that God has given. I am sometimes tempted to be like the third servant who said, "I was afraid" (Verse 25). We hide our talents because we are afraid of failure and what others may think of us, or because hard work and responsibility may be involved.

It has been said that "the greatest mistake people make in life is to be continually fearing they will make one."

The servant who received five talents and the one who received two talents must both have had risks to take. Step out in faith, use your gifts and risk failure.

Jesus says, "in effect, use them or lose them." (Verses 28-30). If you do the very best with what you have, God will give you more and say, "Well done, good and faithful servant. You have been faithful with a few things; I will put you in charge of many things, Come and share your master's happiness." (Verse 21-23)

Our purposes for the Mission are:

- To make the church in a good and clean environment to worship;

- To repair leaky roof and paint ceiling;

- To paint the church inside and outside;

- To build fence around the property to keep the animals away so they can use the land to grow vegetables;

- School feeding program;

- Evangelize, Salvation, Baptism;

- Find full time pastor; and,

- To equip the church with drums, keyboard, guitar, sound system.

My motto for the Mission:

"Do all the good you can
Do all the means you can
In all the ways you can
At all the places you can
At all the times you can
To all the people you can
As long as ever you can."

Our Theme Song:

HEAR THE CALL OF THE KINGDOM
Hear the call to the Kingdom
Lift your eyes to the King
Let His songs rise within you
As a fragrant offering

O how God rich in mercy
Come in Christ to redeem
All who trust in
His unfailing grace

Hear the call of the Kingdom
To be children of light
With the mercy of heaven
The humility of Christ

Walking just before Him
Loving all that is right
That the life of Christ
May shine through us

Chorus
King of heaven
We will answer the call
We will follow
Bringing hope to the world
Filled with passion
Filled with power to proclaim
Salvation in Jesus Name

Hear the call of the Kingdom
To reach out to the lost
With the Father's compassion
In the wonder of the cross

Bringing peace and forgiveness
And a hope yet to come
Let the nations put
their trust in Him.

SECTION 11

Challenges

"I can do all things through Christ
who strengthens me."
Philippians 4:13

The few things that I have learned from these Mission trips are true to life. There are a lot of challenges when you are leading a group, and less challenges when you are just joining a group. Leading a group is a huge responsibility and it is very challenging. When I organized the Mission Trip, I only wrote down my plans and purpose of the trip as far as what the church needed.

I knew someone who is offering her house for us to stay during the length of the volunteers stay. It sounded really good at that time. When I asked how much we need to pay for our stay, she said "nothing." In the end, it turned out that she needed to put an electric pump to get water supply which was going to cost a lot of money, more money if we rented a resort. As we were further discussing the arrangements, it got more complicated. First, there was a problem with water supply. Then, there were not enough beds and bedrooms, not enough washrooms, it's far from the church, and it's one hour away by bus.

So, considering all the issues, I felt that the place was not an appropriate accommodation for the group, but I also did not want to hurt the lady's feelings for not staying at her place.

Also, I have arranged for a Pastor from Cagayan de Oro (CDO) that I met during my previous mission trips because the lead pastor did not have time and was busy with other things. I arranged for this pastor from CDO to go to the Northern part of the Philippines. He stayed at this lady's house. The Pastor made a list of what is required to do a crusade and I sent money for that and they went to buy the necessary stuff. The lady wanted me to install a water pump system in her house, as a "payment" for our stay.

So, when I told the lady that her place is not ideal for us to stay in, she was upset and our relationship was never the same since. It's all about lack of understanding and wrong motive. I was also at fault for committing and agreeing before I searched other options, but I have been away from home for almost 50 years and I didn't know many people or places so I depended on other people to lead me to the right direction.

Then, I found another lady whom I went to High School with who owns a resort in the same town where the church is situated. I contacted her and told her about the group I am bringing to do work for the church. I told her I have a budget and in return, she assured me that she will take care of us. I booked four cottages and I wrote out the quotes she gave me to inform the Board and make sure it's approved by them.

SECTION 12

Fundraising

"But seek first His Kingdom and His righteousness,
and all these things will be given to you as well.
Therefore, do not worry about tomorrow, for
tomorrow will worry about itself.
Each day has enough trouble of its own."
Matthew 6: 33-34

We registered our Ministry in 2019. We applied for Charity, but our application was denied. So, I am doing this work on my own with some support from my children.

In May 29 2019, we organized a fundraising activity with the intention to send a Sea Container to the church's location and to also help us with the mission. It was a success. We had lots of fun, and we got to share what the Lord put into my heart. Being a missionary is a very challenging task, but knowing that God is with me all the time, I have 'no fear' anymore.

Since then, I have not been able to do fundraising because of the Covid Pandemic that restricted a lot of socializing and gathering. Summer of 2021 came. I decided to produce succulents in small containers and sold them in front of my cottage during the summer. I was also doing charity plant sale every year during the summer. This kept my summer busy and interesting. I met a lot of people in my community, and got acquainted with some of them.

This year in 2022, I decided to learn quilting and made baby blankets to sell for charity. I had to put it aside because I believed God wanted me to focus on my book.

Not only that, God reminded me to start and finish writing my book that I have been planning for years, to tell my amazing vision, struggles, challenges and financial provision that God supplied in perfect time. It was an 18-year journey, but by the grace of God, it's coming into a victorious completion.

I am new to writing a book. I have never done it before, but again, I am trusting God to help me through it. To writing, finding a publisher and launching the book, everything was pretty exciting. I can't wait how this turns out. With God's help, I am confident that a lot of people will be ministered and be touched by my personal experience in serving the Lord. He is my ultimate helper in all I do.

SECTION 13

Preparing the Volunteers

The next lesson to the volunteers was to discuss the geography of the Philippines, demographic, economy, education, the exact location we were going, the dialects, the food, the currency etc.

Every month since the conception of my Mission last January 26, 2019, I met with the group to discuss concerns and answer questions that they may have. Also, it is good to prepare them mentally, physically, emotionally and spiritually, and I also saw this as a chance for us to get to know each other, since we will all be a close-knit family for three weeks in a strange country to them. As I have mentioned to my group, it takes nine months to deliver a child from conception. So, full preparation for our mission is very helpful to all of us.

We also discussed where we can visit if time allows.

SECTION 14

Protection: Armor Up

"Put on the whole armor of God that you may be able
to stand against the schemes of the devil."
Ephesians 6:11

Just as we would never travel underwater without scuba equipment, we should not take the Gospel into the world without the armor of God.

> *"Stand therefore, take up the full armor of God, so*
> *that you will be able to resist in the devil day, and*
> *having done everything to stand firm. Stand firm*
> *therefore, having girded your loins with truth, and*
> *having shod your feet with the preparation of the*
> *Gospel of peace; In addition to all, taking up the shield*
> *of faith with which you will be able to extinguish all*
> *the flaming arrows of the evil one. And take His helmet*

of salvation, and the sword of the Spirit, which is the
word of God."
Ephesians 6:14-17

I included all these equipment whenever I went on a Mission.

I remember when we were at the airport leaving for my second Mission Trip, my bag, where my Bibles and devotion journal are, was left behind. I told my son I needed it because my medication was in it. My son had to drive home to get it and it's an hour away for a one way trip. I spoke to the volunteers at the Airport, and told the person who helps people with disability what was happening. The flight waited for me to join the group. I was supposed to board first as a handicap, but I was the last because I could not travel without the armor of God.

Similarly, each part of the armor that Paul described in *Ephesians 6:13-17* is necessary to help us successfully complete God's mission in our lives.

These precious coverings, these spiritual tools, aid us in deflecting the darts of the enemy so we can bring forth God's plans and kingdom.

This armor does not weigh us down; it enables us to thrive in our mission to minister the kingdom of light.

SECTION 15

Leading Strong

Leaders don't boast!

All of us, every leader, no matter how great, will be tempted to be boastful. Every single one! No exception!

> *"Then God remembered Rachel, and God gave heed to*
> *her. So, she conceived and bore a son and said, 'God*
> *has taken away my reproach.' She named him Joseph,*
> *saying 'May the Lord give me another son.'"*
> *Genesis 30:22-24*

> *"Joseph, when he was seventeen years of age, was*
> *pasturing the flock with his brothers while he was*
> *still a youth, along with the sons of Bilhah, the sons*
> *Zilpah, his father's wives. Joseph brought back a bad*
> *report about them to their father. Now, Israel loved*
> *Joseph more than all his sons, because he was the son*

of his old age; and he made him a varicolored tunic.
His brother's saw that their father loved him more
than all his brothers; and they hated him and could
not speak to him on friendly terms. Then Joseph had a
dream, and when he told it to his brothers, they hated
even more.
He said to them, 'Please listen to this dream which I
had; for behold, we were binding sheaves in the field,
and lo, my sheaf rose up and also stood erect; and
behold, your sheaves gathered around and bowed
down to my sheaf.'
Then his brothers said to him, 'Are you actually going
to reign over us?' So, they hated him even more for his
dreams and for his words."
Genesis 37:2-8

So, the story of Joseph with his fabulous coat and his dreams of ruling over his family was no different to all of us. Every leader, no matter how great we are, will be tempted to be boastful. Every. Single. One.

The way in which we talk matters too. There is a very thin line between celebrating and boasting. How can we, as leaders, keep ourselves from boasting, especially in this Social Media world?

Firstly, do a heart check. Ask yourself: "Why am I sharing this?"

Sometimes, we need to take a moment and get gut-level honest with ourselves about our motives before we speak, share, or hit send. "Am I posting for encouragement? Do I share for celebration? Am I seeking to make myself look better?"

Secondly, do a filter check. Ask yourself: "Is there a better way to be sharing this?"

Even with right motivations, we can still miss the delivery. "I should take a second look at that photo before it invades Instagram." "Reread that comment before it is shot out through my text messages." "Think twice about that story before my lips get ahead of my brain."

People don't want to follow a boastful leader. In fact, just like Joseph's brothers, bragging may lead to nothing but the building up of resentment in their hearts. Let's be leaders who are willing to consistently check our hearts and filters to ensure that we don't boast.

SECTION 16

Salvation

"Ho, everyone who thirst, come to the waters; and you who have no money come, buy and eat. Come buy wine and milk, without money and without cost. Why do you spend money for what is not bread, and your wages for what does not satisfy? Listen carefully to Me, and eat what is good, and delight yourself with abundance. Incline your ear and come to Me. Listen that you may live, and I will make an everlasting covenant with you, according to the faithful mercies shown to David."
Isaiah 55:1-3

SALVATION is the act of saving someone from sin or evil; something that may save someone, or something from danger or a difficult situation.

We receive salvation in Christ through repentance and faith. This means: turning away from sinful ways (repentance), turning to God (faith), and trusting Christ. Jesus will forgive your sins and set you on a path to life with Him. We cannot earn this right; it is His free gift.

"Giving your life to Jesus changes everything. Jesus came to reveal who God is and to restore a relationship with him. No matter your past mistakes or your present fears, Jesus can give you a new life. In Him all you need to do is put your faith and trust in Him."

The Bible says:

> "if you declare with your mouth that Jesus is Lord and
> believe in your heart that God raised him from the
> dead, you will be saved".
> Romans 10:9

It is turning from our old ways and turning to Jesus, to ask Him for forgiveness from our sins and to give us new life in Him.

Say a prayer from your heart. "God I know that I have sinned. I am reaching out to you because I want forgiveness. I believe that you died, you were buried, and on the third day you rose again and appeared. I trust in Jesus and Jesus alone as my personal Lord and Saviour. Thank you Lord for forgiving me and saving me. Amen".

SECTION 17

Journey Begins

Prior to our departure, on October 31, 2019, a willow tree fell on my house due to a terrible storm. This did not stop me from leaving to the Mission Trip. Sometimes, the devil wants to distract you or to stop you from going to reach your goal. Not me! I know that God will take care of it and God will be with us throughout our journey.

> *"And we know that God causes all things to work together for good to those who love God, to those who are called according to His purpose."*
> *Romans 8:28*

Finally, November 6, 2019 came and we boarded Philippine Airlines which is a direct flight to Manila. It was a 15-hour direct flight to Manila Airport. We had two SUVs waiting for us to go to Ilocos Sur. It was about 10-12 hours travel to reach our final destination. We stopped to eat a few times on the way. It was a very long and tiring journey but we were all making jokes and enjoying the journey and the scenery.

It was rice-planting season and we saw a lot of farmers wearing hats in the field while planting rice under the very hot sun.

November 8, 2019, we arrived at the Resort to check in at 4:30 pm. Upon arrival, there was a confusion with our reservation. The owner, my friend, was not there. We were advised to pick any cottage, which we did. Then, we went out to the mall and ate at Mang Inasal, ordered chicken inasal and the famous Halo- Halo (crushed ice with preserved fruits and beans with evaporated milk). It's very famous and is one of our delicacies.

November 9, 2019
On the first day, we went to evangelize door-to-door in pairs. One pair went to a house and prayed for a lady who is dying of Cancer. Her daughter is from Toronto, and she is a Christian. We went to pray for my nephew who was suffering from pancreatic cancer. His wife, the daughter, and a young girl received Jesus as their personal Savior. Praise God!

November 10, 2019
We were welcomed to do church service at Rayma Worship Center.

When we arrived at RWC, there was no one in the church, no attendees. The fear came upon me. Then we started worshipping. Out of the blue, people started coming in. It was a very good service. But after the service, they wanted to feed all the people who attended. Apparently, this is their tradition here, but I disagree with that tradition. It cost money, and it would deplete the purpose of having a church service. In my opinion, we are giving the wrong message. The purpose for people to go to church is to come and hear the message and received the Word of God, and not to eat food.

SALVATION

"Now it happened that the crowd was pressing around
Him and listening to the word of God, He was stand-
ing by the lake of Gennesaret; and He saw two boats
lying at the edge of the lake: but the fishermen got out
of them and were washing their nets. And He got into
one of the boats, which was Simon's, and asked him to
put out a little way from the land. And He sat down
and began teaching the people from the boat. When
He had finished speaking, He said to Simon, 'Put out
into the deep water and let down your nets for a catch.'
Simon answered and said, 'Master, we worked hard
all night and caught nothing, but I will do as you say
and let down the nets.' When they had done this, they
enclosed a great quantity of fish, and their nets began
to break. So, they signaled to their partners in the
other boat for them to come and help them. And they
came and filled both of the boats, so that they began
to sink. But when Simon Peter saw that, he fell down
to Jesus' feet, saying, 'Go away from me, for I am a
sinful man!' For amazement had seized him and all
his companions because of the catch of fish which they
had taken; and so also were James and John, sons of
Zebedee, who were partners with Simon. And Jesus
said to Simon, 'Do not fear from me; from now on you
will be catching men.'"
Luke 5:1-11

This has been one of my favorite verses even when I was with
Usana trying to get people to try the premium quality vitamins.
But today, this became more alive within my spirit, "you will be
catching men" to save the lost!

See, there was no one at the church and I was afraid and also disappointed. It's natural to feel this way. But, when Jesus is at your side and you obey what Jesus tells you to do, situations and circumstances change. When you obey and trust Jesus, great things happen.

Then, I saw people come in. They repented and received Jesus as their personal Savior. These people became new creations, their old lives are gone. Praise God! These people are free!

Firstly, obeying Jesus is very important and is the key to prosperity and progress. On the other hand, disobedience causes us to break down.

Secondly, change is also important. The story of the fishermen is a great example. They were professional fishermen, they thought, but changing the location to throw the net made a big difference. They caught a great quantity of fish and it overflowed. It can also happen to your life if you are willing to follow Jesus and obey.

This is my proof and key to fulfill God's vision in my life.

SALVATION was preached by one of the volunteers.

Twelve people accepted Jesus as their personal Savior. Their old lives are gone and they are now born-again Christians. They are brand new creations.

During the PM service, eight more souls were saved and got baptized. Praise God! This was an amazing day that the Lord hath made. We rejoiced and became glad in it.

SECTION 18

Water Baptism

Water baptism symbolizes the believer's total trust in and total reliance on the Lord Jesus Christ, as well as a commitment to live obediently to HIM.

*"Water baptism is a beautiful picture of what our Lord
has done for us. As we are completely immersed in the
water, we symbolize the burial with our Lord; we are
baptized into His death on the cross and are
no longer slaves to sin."*
Romans 6:3-7

*"When we are raised out of the water, we are symboli-
cally resurrected- raised to new life in Christ to be with
Him forever, both into the family of our loving God."*
Romans 8:16

Water baptism also illustrates the spiritual cleansing experience we encounter when we are saved; just as water cleanses the flesh, so the Holy Spirit cleanses our hearts when we trust Christ.

"Christians should be baptized out of obedience
to and love for our Lord Jesus."
John 14:15

Water baptism by immersion is a biblical method of baptism because of its symbolic representation of the death, burial, and resurrection of Christ.

I remember when I got baptized in the Jordan River in 2007, my husband and I joined a group tour with Bethel Gospel Tabernacle. Water baptism was not in our itinerary. I have not been baptized after I got saved. So, I privately asked the pastor's wife if there is any way I could be baptized in Jordan River. She told me she will try and persuade the pastor, but she can't promise anything. I left it as that. Then, we boarded in the bus in the morning and the next thing I knew, she was asking for people who wanted to be baptized at the Jordan River. My heart jumped up from joy. I asked my husband if he wants to get baptized, but he refused. There were eight people who got baptized that day. It was one of the happiest days in my life. After the baptism, my husband did not talk to me for a couple of days. He was upset, but I was obeying what God wants me to do. If I disobeyed God, I don't know where I would be today. That is what I believed in. God first, then your husband and family. Husbands can forget about it after few days, but with God, it's forever. This was not my priority before I got saved. It was my husband first, then my family and God as my last! I'm ashamed!

Today, we had a total of 20 baptisms. PRAISE GOD!!!

SECTION 19

First School Feeding Program

We brought some dried vegetables donated by Gleaners of Canada. The kitchen staff of the school made some soup and muffins from the dried vegetable. The recipes were created by Filipino people in CDO, who has been using the products for many years. It was a hit!

126 children were fed.

Activities:

- Basketball. Zoe did a three-point shot. The children picked her up in the air and cheered on her. The children loved Daniela and Zoe.

- Girls: hair braiding by Zoe and Daniela

- Boys: rope tying lesson by one of the volunteers.

- Bead demonstration (each color symbolizes something different)

Black=sin	Yellow= promise
Red= blood of Jesus	Blue= baptism
White= purity	Green= growth

SECOND SCHOOL FEEDING PROGRAM

November 12, 2019

We used the same dried vegetable product but in different recipes. This product is very versatile and healthy. They have some malnourished children in school, and also children who have no food to eat before going to school, that it affects their school performances. Feeding program is also ideal for this school.

Activities:

- Personal hygiene by one of the volunteers
- Games created by Zoe and Daniela

These two Schools wanted me to support them with the feeding program using the dried vegetables that we brought from Canada. We had the agreements done, but due to Covid, we were not able to proceed. I will do a follow up on my next Mission Trip.

SECTION 20

Crusade

November 13, 2019

I felt the division and tension that night. The Senior Pastor came with his members but I felt the distance and coldness of some adults in the village. I was not sure why. The adults segregated themselves and did not participate in the activities at all, but the children were so happy and excited. They participated very well with the activities. One of the volunteers did a sign light presentation. Two ladies from the group sang with a guitar accompaniment.

Some volunteers did a puppet show with Zoe and Daniela.

There was also a basketball shooting competition. We gave away Bibles as prices to some of the games and contests.

During the week, we all went to do physical work at the church. Some painted, while some cleaned the whole place. Repair of the roof and ceiling were done by experienced laborers in the area. I met the Barangay Captain and he arranged for me to drop some blankets that I brought from Canada to the Narvacan Hospital, which was very much appreciated. I got a tour of the Hospital by one of the Nurses in charge. Patients were in the hallways; lying on a lawn chair, sitting on the floor, and the hospital was very congested. The hospital is still in need of a lot of equipment, electric beds, chairs, stretchers, linens, and more.

SECTION 21

Tour

November 16, 2019

We all decided to take a day off. We rented a van and we all went to Laoag, Ilocos Norte. It took us six hours to arrive there. We visited Fort Ilocandia Resort, Malacañang Palace of the North, Paoay, St Augustine Church, and we had dinner at Regency Hotel.

FORT ILOCANDIA RESORT

It is the only 5-star deluxe resort hotel in Northern Philippines sprawling over 77 hectares of land amidst gentle sand dunes and fine forest with a 2-kilometer sandy beach facing China Sea.

This was originally constructed by Marcos Family for their daughter Irene's wedding reception.

Ilocandia Golf and Country Club was built in 1978 in Ilocos Norte. Ever since its construction, it has been one of the pride and joys of the Ilocos area.

MALACANANG PALACE

One of the most visited places in Ilocos Norte is the renowned Malacañang of the North or Malacañang Amianan (North) as the locals refer it to. Today, it is grand mansion with beautiful grounds and overlooking a lake maintained by the local government of the province.

About Malacañang of the North:

The Malacañang of the North is a presidential museum in Paoay, Ilocos Norte, Philippines. It was the residence of the family of Ferdinand Marcos when he was a president of the Philippines. This was a birthday gift from the first lady, Imelda Marcos, to her husband for his 60th birthday. It was named after the official residence and workplace of the President of the Philippines in Manila- the Malacañang Palace.

It is among a number of properties belonging to the Marcos family which were sequestered by the Philippine Government when President Marcos Sr. was removed from power.

After 20 years of ownership by the government, the property was eventually given back to the jurisdiction of Ilocos Norte. Restoration and renovations were commenced by the region's Governor, and in 2011 the property and grounds were opened up to public as a museum.

My story regarding the founding of the RWC was a little similar to it. When I bought it in 2008, it changed hands of ownership. The restoration took place in 2011 and now it's open to the public for worship.

Do you think it's coincidental? I believe that this is God's plan to show that no matter how little our dream or breakthrough is, there is only God who we thank for it. I thank my God for every little thing, every little miracle that He gives me every day. For the *"big and small miracles, are worth celebrating for His goodness and faithfulness."*

ST AUGUSTIN CHURCH or SIMBAHAN NG PAOAY

Church History:

Paoay church was founded by Augustinian missionaries in 1593 and was a labor of love over time and in the face of earthquakes and other disasters.

The Paoay Church history began in the 17th century. What started out as a Paoay Church drawing turned into reality. The construction of the church in Ilocos Norte was over a century, which began in 1604, the cornerstone of the church was laid in 1704, the convent in 1707, and the bell-tower in 1793. Even while still unfinished, Paoay Church was already used by parishioners. In 1896, it was finally inaugurated, but in 1706 and 1927, it was damaged by earthquakes.

Its scars made it more beautiful and worth visiting. Because of St. Augustin Church Paoay's historical and artistic significance, it was designed as a National Culture Treasure by the Philippine government in 1973 and Unesco World Heritage Site among county's baroque church in 1993.

Seeing this in person, you would think that it's like a postcard. The sky above the church is often a deep cerulean, making it a photographer's haven.

Paoay Church has an interesting design overall. It is adorned with eight pilasters and twenty-four extravagant coral-block buttresses and ornate stone finials that hold it up and protect it against earthquake damage.

The bell tower was intended to be constructed at a distance from the church to minimize damage, should it fall.

According to historians, the bell tower served as a status symbol for the locals- the bell would ring more loudly and more times during the wedding of a prominent clan than it would during the wedding of the less privileged. It was also said to have been used as a Filipino watchtower during 1898 uprising against Spaniards.

Its altar and retablo are of plain design compared to others; the latter bears an only a statue of the church patron saint, San Augustin. Nevertheless, it doesn't diminish the church's beauty.

I wish that one day, RWC will become a historical place for people for fellowship and place to worship God, and a storehouse for the saved and unsaved.

REGENCY HOTEL IN VIGAN

We were given a delicious and special meal, courtesy of the owner of Regency Hotel. We also had full body massage at a very reasonable prize. It was a lovely dinner and very good time together; just exploring and taking a break from our very busy schedule.

SECTION 22

Sunday Service

November 17,2019

- 9:30 service preached by the guest pastor;
- Guest pastor did the altar call of salvation;
- 20 youth accepted Jesus as their personal Savior; and
- 20 baptisms at Paraiso ni Juan.

It was a glorious morning! Praise God.

The volunteers were pretty tired to come to the afternoon service. Plus, our guest pastor was not feeling well. Satan was not happy to see what is happening at the church. He was attacking the visiting pastor and the volunteers, but we will not stop.

There were only three of us going to the afternoon service where the Lead pastor usually have the service time. When we arrived at that specified time of service, no one was there except for the workers who were building the fence around the property. My lady friend who has a close connection with the lead pastor's team tried to message the team, and she was told that they were already in the village, having the service somewhere else. There was no communication between me and the senior pastor team since we arrived, not even a welcome greeting to the missionaries. I didn't know the reason why. I made two attempts to meet with the senior pastor, but he never showed up. I had a feeling that this was already planned to betray me and Rayma Worship Center.

SECTION 23

Betrayal

"For, it is not an enemy, who reproaches me. Then,
I could bear it; nor is it one who hates me who has
exalted himself against me, Then I could hide myself.
But it is you, a man my equal, my companion and my
familiar friend; We who had sweet fellowship together
walked in the house of God in the throng."
Psalm 55:12-14

Jesus knows how it feels. He was betrayed twice.
Quote:

"The saddest thing about betrayal is that it never
comes from your enemies."

Being betrayed by a friend, family, or fellow Christians is one of
the worst feelings ever. Sometimes, the emotional pain is far worse

than that of physical pain. The question I had at that moment is "How should I handle betrayal?" The first thing my flesh wanted to do, is get revenge. If not physically, then in my mind.

We must be still. As quoted in Psalms, *"Be still and know I am God."*

We must take our minds off the situation and put our focus on Christ. If we keep thinking about the situation, then it will only build up anger.

We must give our problems to the Lord. He will calm the storm within us.

We must follow the example of Christ who was also betrayed twice.

Let's forgive others. We must rest upon the Spirit.

We must ask the Spirit to help us love our enemies and to remove any bitterness and anger lurking in our hearts.

Understand that all the difficult things we face in life, God will use it for His great purpose. Just as Joseph in our previous section said, *"you meant evil against me, but God meant it for good."*

When we set our minds on Christ, there is an amazing peace and feeling of love that He will provide.

Go and find a quiet place. Cry out to God. Allow God to help your pain and hurt. Pray for your betrayer just like Christ prayed for His enemies.

It's funny that the morning message was about betrayal; Peter, betraying Jesus on His last day. God was showing me things that I needed to know. It's a true revelation, and I thank God for it.

My declaration is, *"the battles of life are perfecting me. I am learning to know and trust God and to know myself."*

My second betrayal was when I went to settle my account with the resort. My "friend" was charging me twice as much as we have agreed upon. I did not have the confirmation from her regarding what we discussed on the phone, but I had my notes, and my two volunteers knew the cost during our meeting prior to leaving. They stood up and fought for me. We paid for Wi-Fi that did not work at all.

Some of the group left for the Airport on November 21 by bus. The other two members and the guest pastor went to Cagayan de Oro to do more Missions. They have gone there in the past, and they plan to come back to Ilocos.

After the group left, I stayed at my friend's house as she insisted for me to stay with her until the other two missionaries comes back from CDO. My friend wanted us to stay at her house until they are ready to return to Canada. I hired a driver to come pick me up every day to go to church which is forty-five minutes, away and back. It was costing me a lot of money for transportation, one reason why this location was not ideal.

While I was on my own, I did more evangelizing. My driver met a friend at a money exchange store and found out that his friend was very sick. We went to visit and pray for the whole family. The whole family of five got saved, received Jesus as their personal Savior. Then, the whole family showed up in church that Sunday. They also got baptized.

November 24 Sunday service.
During the 9:30 service, there was no pastor. The Guest Pastor left to CDO.

I did the service. We have few church members in attendance. Nine children from my village attended. Some youth did the worship songs.

During the 3:30 service, Tessie and Marcelo came from Santa to do the service. The rest of the children that we met on the road said, *"Hi lola(grandma) Betty"*, and I said *"Hi mga anak (children),"* I asked, *"Why don't you come to church anymore?"* and they answered, *"because our parents don't allow us."* I find it very disturbing.

SECTION 24

Food Distributions to Elderly Low-Income People

December 2 to December 13, 2019

Every day, we went with municipal staff to distribute bags of food to 32 Barangays in Narvacan. We distributed to 50 recipients. The list of recipients who were eligible to receive the bag of food was provided by the Municipality staff. It was very sad and heart breaking to see how these elderly people were living alone in a very small spaces they occupy with just a few belongings. But when they received the bag of blessings, their smiles were price-less. They were so grateful and thankful that we went to see them. These are the kind of people you don't mind helping. They are so appreciative for the little bag they received.

It has been two Sundays without a preacher. I was very worried and discouraged, but I continued to pray and hope that God will provide a pastor in His perfect time.

The fence was almost done. In the meantime, I was still staying alone at my friend's big house in Santa. It was very lonely and depressing, but it provided more time to seek God for guidance and direction on where to find a pastor. My friend was never home. She left me alone in her house.

Tessie and Marcelo live next door to my friend's house. They are related to my friend. They are very nice and understanding, and they feel my pain. They are like a family to me, which I am very thankful for. We cooked and have our suppers together. They come to Rayma Worship Center's service on Sundays when they can. I thank both of them for their kindness, love, and support they have given me during my difficult trials, struggles, and problems that I was facing. They were there for me, encouraging me. I also encouraged them with their trials in their relationship.

Tessie and Marcelo were doing children's ministry to a small group of children that were left at Rayma Worship Center. We were doing our best to keep the church alive.

On December 7, Marcelo and Tessie invited Mark, Lily, and myself to attend their church in Labut and to meet Pastor Bong. We did not have service at Rayma Worship Center in Abour, because we did not have a pastor for three weeks now. Pastor Bong gave a powerful message. I invited him to come and speak the following Sunday, Dec. 15, and on Dec. 17, during the Christmas Party celebration.

The pain and worry of not having a pastor around Christmas was very gut-wrenching. My own family lived thousands of miles away, but God puts another family in my life to comfort me and support me. I consider Marcelo and Tessie and my cousins Pedro and Loling as my family in the Philippines. I still have a lot of cousins and distant relatives but it is very different.

Marcelo and Tessie are the ones who introduced me to Pastor Bong, their pastor. Thank God that Pastor Bong and his wife Amelia agreed to come and do services at Rayma Worship Center.

More importantly, I thank God my Savior for answering my urgent request for a temporary pastor to service the needs of Rayma Worship Center. God is always with me! He never leaves me nor forsakes me! I put my trust in Him! He holds the future of Rayma Worship Center and He is in control of my life. In all I do, I depend on Him, on Him alone!

SECTION 25

God's Presence

"But now, thus says the Lord, your creator, O Jacob,
and He who formed you, O Israel, "Do not fear, for I
have redeemed you; I have called you by name: you
are Mine! When you pass through the waters, I will be
with you; And through the rivers, they will not over-
flow you. When you walk through the fire, you will not
be scorched, nor will the flame burn you."
Isaiah 43:1-2

What words of encouragement from the Lord? *"Do not fear,*
for I have redeemed you". He redeemed me for sure; from my
struggles, trials and circumstances. He also said, *"I will be with*
you". What an amazing feeling that I was not alone in my struggles
and pain? He was and will always be with me.

When God's presence is with you, you may pass through deep
waters, but they will not overflow. You won't drown. You may be

forced to walk into the fiery furnace but you won't be burned. You may be thrown into a lion den, but the animals will not harm you. They may prowl around, roar and try to intimidate, but they can't harm you. Hallelujah!

When God's Presence is with you, you will be able to face prophets of Baal and emerge victorious. You will be able to confront criticizing, backbiting, rebellious people. You will be able to courageously advance into enemy territory with authority because you know you cannot be defeated; in the prison, in the ghetto, on gang turf, in the drug dens!

You can march right in and rescue people from the very gates of Hell because you have the ultimate weapon: God's Divine Presence!

With God's Presence leading you, you can go through flood, you can go through any fire, you can go through any trials, and you will come through victorious because His presence is with you.

December 15, 2019
We had our first celebration with Pastor Bong since we arrived in November. It was such a powerful and anointed service. There were about thirty people in attendance. Praise the Lord!

I really felt the Presence of the Lord in the church. Praise God! I believed that Rayma Worship Center is going to be a Church of God and His Presence.

God's Presence equips us with saving and keeping power. It provides guiding power. His Presence strengthens us and separates us from the world. It heals, renews, and cleanses us… It is unlimited power! That is why we must have His Presence!

"For this reason I bow my knees before the Father,
from whom every family in heaven and on earth
derives its name that He would grant you, according to
the riches of His glory, to be strengthened with power
through His Spirit in the inner man, so that Christ

may dwell in your hearts through faith; and that, you being rooted and grounded in love, may be able to comprehend with all the saints what the breadth and length and height and depth and to know the love of Christ which surpasses knowledge, that you may be filled up to all the fullness of God. Now to Him who is able to do far more abundantly beyond all that we ask or think, according to the power that works within us, to whom be the glory in the church and in Christ Jesus to all generations forever and ever. Amen."

Ephesians 3:14-23

SECTION 26

A Church Must Have His Presence

When God birthed Rayma Worship Center, He didn't birth another club or organization. He didn't birth Protestants, Catholics, or Iglesia ni Cristo, Jehovah's Witness (not any religion *per se*). God birthed Rayma Worship Center with the intention to generate dynamic forces, a supernatural power that would never experience any limits. God was literally making a deposit of Himself, through Jesus and the Holy Spirit into our bodies.

In the beginning, God walked and talked with Adam. In the Old Testament record, God came upon the prophets and judges to manifest Himself and then after the work is done, His Presence would lift. But when Rayma Worship Center was birthed, God Himself came to indwell His body.

> *"As for you, the anointing you received from Him remains in you, and you have no need for anyone to*

teach you: but as His anointing teaches you about all
things, and is true and is not a lie, and just as it has
taught you, you abide in Him."
1 John 2:27

Christ rules in you permanently. His anointing abides in you permanently. His presence is within you-and it is there to stay.

When you battle with sickness or disease in your body, you know His Presence is there. When you face a financial crisis, or you have a mountain of debt and it keeps piling up, God's Presence is right at your side. When you are in danger, you don't fear because you know His Presence is there. When you are battling fatigue, worry, and depression, you are not dismayed because you know God's Presence is with you.

SECTION 27

God, Show Me Your Glory

December 16,2019
God knows my cry and fervent prayers for His revelation. I needed help guidance and directions from Him. I knew that God sent me to a Mission for a reason and a purpose. I have been praying to find the right pastor for Rayma Worship Center. I have been asking God to show me and reveal to me the right one. Moses said and cried out to God, *"Show me thy glory" (Exodus 33:18).* This was also my prayer until He finds me the right pastor.

Every day, I read my devotion the first thing in the morning, and God always shows me the Scripture to answer my request.

In answer to Moses heart's cry, he received confirmation of God's Presence. God said:

...."my presence shall go with thee,
and I will give thee rest"
Exodus 34:1-8

But God's Presence wasn't enough to satisfy the cry of Moses heart. He did not stop there. Moses pressed on and boldly asked: "*I beseech thee, show me thy glory*".

There is a difference between beholding God's Presence and possessing the glory. Many people go their entire Christian lives without experiencing either of these few presses, and beyond the point of blessing to experience God's Presence and power. Very few, however, persevere to receive a revelation of God's glory.

Moses wanted more than just God's Presence. He wanted His guidance, provision, blessing and power. This wasn't enough for him. He wanted a manifestation of God's glory. He knew there was more than His Presence and so he cried out, *"show me thy glory"*.

God's glory is what I needed at this point. Not only His presence, but His guidance, provision, blessing, and power. I prayed for guidance as to where I may find peace and prayed that I would find the right pastor, in order to pursue His blessing and power.

> *"Then Moses said to the Lord, 'See, you say to me,*
> *bring up this people!' But You Yourself have not let*
> *me know whom You will send with me. Moreover,*
> *You have said, 'I have known you by name, and you*
> *have also found favor in My sight.' 'Now therefore, I*
> *pray to You, if I have found favor in Your sight, let me*
> *know Your ways that I may know You, so that I may*
> *find favor in Your sight. Consider too, that this nation*
> *(Narvacan) is Your people."*
> *Exodus 33:12-13*

This was my daily prayer and request to God. Because He told me, "Build me a church." I needed Him to show me His ways to how. I needed His guidance, His blessing, His provision and His power to complete the task He has given me. I know I can't do it alone. It is impossible in my eyes, but with God all things are possible!

WHEN GOD'S GLORY IS REVEALED

"He said, 'If now I have found favor in Your sight, O Lord, I pray, let the Lord go along in our midst, even though the people are so obstinate, and pardon our iniquity and our sin, and take us as Your own possession,' Then God said, 'Behold, I am going to make a covenant. Before all your people I will perform miracles, which has not been produced in all the earth nor among any of the nations; and all the people among whom you live will see the working of the Lord, for it is a fearful thing that I am going to perform with you.'"
Exodus 34:9-10

This Scripture spoke to me clearly; I needed to ask for forgiveness of my sin and my inequities. God has promised me that He will perform a miracle which has not been produced in all the earth. If God promised something, He will do. I am confident that God will find me the right pastor for Rayma Worship Center.

SECTION 28

Year 2020: New Beginning

For all that is unknown about a New Year, one thing that I know for sure is that new days are on their way. Whether I am the one who feels like I am running out of time, or I am excited about what's to come, I trust that every hour of this New Year 2020 would be wrapped in endless, boundless race.

So, whether we are looking forward to a New Year with hope, worry, gratitude, or a mixture of things, may we each be reminded all by grace; there is an invitation to talk to God about these things. Every day is an opportunity to carry on faithfully to the journey. Trusting that the love of Christ reminds us how glorious "new" beginnings can be.

My prayer:

Dear Heavenly Father,
Slowly but surely, I am learning to not be afraid of
the wait anymore, for I know, you will open doors;

*beautiful and perfect in their time. I will go deeper
into embracing the process. I will trust that I am not
forgotten. I will lean into the Promise that the Love I
know in Christ is Eternal.
In my despair, I have not been abandoned.
I do not know how much longer I will have to wait for
the right pastor, but I know You are with me.
In Your grace, I am guided right where I am meant to
be. And even when I feel lost on the inside of my mind,
I will trust Your Holy Spirit is still my
ever-faithful guide.
I am not alone on this journey even in the waiting.
I am wholly Yours and I will continue to trust as I wait
for open doors. In Jesus Name!
Amen.*

As I reflect on what God has done for me in 2019, I am so thankful to the God that I serve that He was always with me. He never left me alone. He guided me, He protected me, He provided all I needed exceedingly and abundantly. He provided a place for me to stay when everyone else rejected me. He guided my path every single day. He always directed me to the right path. His Presence was with me all the time.

In 2019, I gained spiritual strength and increased confidence on my vision for God. I now know that the vision God gave me 18 years ago, saying *"build me a church"*, is definitely from Him. There is no doubt in my mind.

My obedience to God made it happen.

Most importantly, there were many souls that were saved, got baptized and walking with the Lord in Narvacan today. We still have a lot of work to do. More workers are needed. I invite you to use your talents for the Lord. Connect with your local church in your area and offer your sacrifice to the Lord. You will be blessed.

In 2019, I also missed a lot of family time which is a part of my sacrifice to serve God.

These are the following special occasions I missed:

- Tyler's 25th birthday in November
- Austin's 21st birthday in December
- Christmas Day
- New Year's Day
- Rowena's 45th birthday in January
- Zoe's 15th birthday in January
- My 75th birthday in January
- Wedding anniversary in February
- December 31st my nephew with pancreatic cancer died.

I wondered what else could go wrong. But I considered all these as blessings.

With the struggles I had for the accommodation of missionaries, God put it into my heart to build a Mission House and bigger Sanctuary as the existing sanctuary is becoming congested.

NEW VISION
NEW SANCTUARY
NEW MISSION HOUSE

SECTION 29

New Beginning

January 2020

January launches the first thirty-one days of a brand-new year. Ahead of us lies the "unknown": What trials will we face this year? What victories awaits us? What changes occur throughout the world? How will our personal lives, our ministries, and our families be impacted in the coming months?

As we pause to reflect on the coming days of this year, we are much like God's people, Israelites, who came to the border of the Promised Land. Ahead of them lay the "unknown" -a land they had not scanned, an enemy they had not accessed. There were tremendous blessings ahead, but there were also some battles that awaited them on the other side of Jordan. The same is true for us.

God instructed Israel to follow closely behind the Ark of the Tabernacle, which was symbolic of His presence in the midst of His people. He told them, *"Do not come near it, that you may know* the way by which you shall go, for you have not passed this way before." (Joshua 3:4)

As we think about the coming year, we too "have not been this way before." We do not know what joys and sorrows, victories and problems, are ahead. But one thing this is for sure; we have the same words of assurance that God gave to Joshua at the border of Canaan. "Have I not commanded you? Be strong and courageous. Do not be afraid: do not be discouraged for the Lord your God will be with you wherever you go."

God has promised to be with us wherever we go. He has commanded us to be strong and of good courage and not to be dismayed. The presence of God is advancing before us into the coming year, just as the Ark led Israel into the "unknown" territory that lay before them.

During the month of January, we will join Israel when they first came to the border of the Promised Land and turned back in defeat. Then we will return with them the second time, when they obeyed God's command to advance and entered in, conquered the enemy and claimed their God's given possession.

There are some exciting times ahead for us as we look to the future with faith. God has tremendous victories planned for us in the coming days. I believe it and receive it! There are some major challenges ahead also, but we are well able to conquer it. He will bring us into the land and give it to us...

> "Then Caleb quieted the people before Moses and said,
> 'We should by all means go up and take possession of
> it, for we will surely overcome it.'"
> Numbers 13:30, 14:8

> "If the Lord is pleased with us, then He will bring us
> into this land and give it to us—a land which flows
> with milk and honey."

I was expecting more challenges ahead but I believe I can conquer it with God's help.

SECTION 30

New Opportunities

January 5, 2020

There was a church service initiated by Pastor Bong. I was feeling discouraged due to lack of attendance. Only eight children and two adults were in attendance.

> *"And with whom was He angry for forty years? Was it*
> *with those who sinned, whose bodies fell in the wilder-*
> *ness? And to whom did He swear that they would not*
> *enter His 'rest', but to those who were disobedient?*
> *So, we see that they were not able to enter*
> *because of unbelief."*
> *Hebrew 3; 17-19*

The word "rest" referred to by apostle Paul here is not referring simply to a place of physical rest from all our labors. It is not a place where we are free from the problems and cares of this life. It is referring to that powerful spiritual dimension where those who enter have taken full possession of their inheritance. It is a place of peace and security, freedom from fear, worry, and stress, even in the midst of great adversity. It is a place of power and victory over our enemies, a place of joy and commitment, a place where we have ceased from our striving, to walk in our own strength and are walking in God's strength. Enter into His "rest", today.

My prayer today

Lord Jesus, I come to you today that I decree and declare that I will enter into Your rest today despite of what happen. I will experience peace and security; I will be free from worry, from fear, and stress despite the circumstances around me in Jesus Name!
Amen.

SECTION 31

Be Grateful

January 7, 2020

I DON'T FORGET WHAT GOD HAS DONE.

I thank God that He brought me this far-eighteen years (18 years) in the making for the church to be built.

I also want to acknowledge my two daughters, Rayma and Rowena, for not giving up on me. And also, my late husband Michael and my son Michael for their support and assistance in making my vision into reality. I also want to thank God for my wonderful and loving grandchildren: Tyler, Austin and Zoe.

I grew up in a Catholic household and I converted to Anglican religion when I got married. Then in December 3, 2003 I got saved, I confessed my sin and I accepted Jesus as my personal Savior. From that day on, my life changed. I have a very close relationship with Jesus. I got baptized at Jordan River in 2008. It was an amazing experience.

I thank God for the vision He gave me, *"build me a church"*. The Rayma Worship Center restoration started in January 20, 2011. The dedication day was February 15, 2011, also our wedding anniversary.

Also, I want to acknowledge the eight missionaries that came with me in November 2019 to complete the second restoration of Rayma Worship Center and to spread the Gospel. I also want to thank my cousin and my niece, Kate Anne, and Pastor Exodo for their dedication in taking care and managing the church. Our Mission Trip was a success. Everything that we planned to do was completed except the key board and a drum set. Praise God!

SECTION 32

Obedience to God

"Then all the congregation lifted up their voices and cried, and the people wept that night. All the sons of Israel grumbled against Moses and Aaron; and the whole congregation said to them, 'Would that we had died in the land of Egypt! Or would that we had died in this wilderness! Why is the Lord bringing us into this land, to fall by the sword? Our wives and little ones will become plunder; would it not be better for us to return to Egypt?' So they said to one another, 'Let us appoint a leader and return to Egypt'. Then Moses and Aaron fell on their faces in the presence of all the assembly of the congregation of the sons of Israel. Joshua, the son of Nun, and Caleb, the son of Jephunneh, of those who had spied out the land, tore their clothes; and they spoke to all the congregation of the son of Israel, saying, 'The land which we passed

through to spy out is an exceedingly good land. If the
Lord is pleased with us, then He will bring us into
this land and give it to us-a land which flows with
milk and honey. Only do not rebel against the Lord;
and do not fear the people of the land, for they will
be our prey. Their protection has been removed from
them, and the Lord is with us; do not fear them.' 'I will
smite them with pestilence and dispossess them, and
I will make you into a nation greater and mightier
than they.'"
Numbers 14: 1-12

I declare that Narvacan is exceedingly good land. Narvacan is a land that flows milk and honey.

"Israel through their unbelief, disobedience and failed
to enter the 'rest' God has planned for them. Paul
warned the believers, 'Let us, therefore, make every
effort to enter that rest, so that no one will fail by
following their example of disobedience.'"
Hebrew 4:11

The only way to enter the powerful spiritual dimensions God has planned for us is through faith and obedience. You must shut out every voice of unbelief that would tempt or deceive you into disobeying God. You must set your heart and mind to obey God, regardless of the cost, like friendship.

The Israelites refused to listen to the voice of God, but chose instead to listen to negative reports. Their hearts were so filled with unbelief they began to grumble and murmur against Moses and Aaron.

There was a lot of complaining and murmuring here also.

Their murmuring and grumbling were directed to us missionaries, but their murmuring was actually against God. It was an onward manifestation of the unbelief that was in their hearts. They had murmured about lack of food.

They had murmured and complained that there was no water. They were not satisfied with the manna God gave them and had murmured and complained that there was no flesh.

God heard their murmuring and was filled with wrath against them. The constant murmuring was a means of accusing Him of not fulfilling His promise to them. They were turning their backs on Him and were forgetting what He had done for them.

How about you? Are you murmuring and complaining because of your circumstances today? Are you turning your back on Him and forgetting what He has done for you at the cross? If so… make this declaration, "I will stop murmuring and complaining. I will not forget what God has done in the past."

SECTION 33

Sickness and Homesick

January 8, 2020

Another attack from the enemy came: I developed a bad cough that is not going away. I have been exposed to a lot of people from watching the body of my nephew who died from pancreatic cancer. I went to the hospital had Xray done and it showed Pneumonia. So, I was on bedrest and on Antibiotics. I also was feeling homesick, missing my children and grandchildren. It was my 75th birthday on January 19. I was very sad, lonely and I felt homesick.

January 20, 2019

As I reflected on what my purpose of my Mission was, I feel I was making progress. There were numerous salvations and baptisms, the church has been restored, and the fence around the building is complete. I bought a guitar but was unable to buy the drum and keyboard.

My biggest worry was finding the right pastor for Rayma Worship Center. Pastor Bong was trying to help me find one. I am trusting on the Lord that He will provide and find one on His perfect time. I have till March 18, 2020 to find one, otherwise the work that we have done will be useless and down the drain without a pastor.

I can't help doubting. I believe, but…

SECTION 34

Do Not Doubt

*"Abram believed the Lord, and He credited it
to him as righteousness."*
Genesis 15:6

*"Do not fear, Abram. I am a shield to you;
your reward shall be very great."*
Genesis 15:1

*God promised to Abram that he will make him a
great nation, but he had no children. God graciously
reassured Abram that a son was coming.*

In this Scripture, it reminded me that I am focused on the physical aspects, what my eyes could see and what my mind could comprehend. It seems so impossible. God told me to build a church, but I have no pastor. What is a church without a devoted pastor? What is a church without a shepherd to take care of the sheep?

I also believe that God gave me the gracious reassurance that a pastor is coming to Rayma Worship Center.

I have gone through three pastors since the birth of Rayma Worship Center.

God was saying to me; "Do not fear"

Without any change of circumstances, Scripture says, that I believe the Lord. I believed God would do what He said He would do. That is my faith.

Faith does not mean we never doubt or have questions. In fact, Abraham (Abram) immediately began asking God how the things, which He spoke of, were possible.

> *"He said to him, 'O Lord God how may*
> *I know that I will possess it?'"*
> *Genesis 15:8*

There is a same question I have for God." How do I know I will find it?"

God promises are eternal and unchangeable. They will not fail because God cannot fail.

We have two choices: we can believe the enemy, or we can believe God.

Choosing lies and self-satisfaction leads to negative consequences. Choosing truth and humility leads to blessing and fulfillment. Why? Because when we choose to believe lies, we fall into the hands of the enemy. We hear the devils voice instead of God's, so He determines who we are, our paths, and even our destiny.

When we trust ourselves or others over God, we risk moving so far from God that we forget His heart, His goodness, and His love. We forget God's commands are good.

Trusting in and obeying God's Word is where we find our true and lasting significance, satisfaction and security.

MY PRAYER

Heavenly Father,
My creator, who art in heaven hallowed be thy name.
Let your will be done. Let your kingdom come.
I praise You that I am fearfully and wonderfully made.
I thank you that I am forgiven and redeemed by the
precious blood of Your Son, Jesus Christ. Thank you
that in and through the power of your Holy Spirit, I
am a new creation. Because of your grace and mercy, I
am your hand-crafted masterpiece and you have good
and perfect purpose for me. Please grant me wisdom
and discernment as I walk out that plan and vision.
Help me to discover who you have created me to be.
Expose the lies of the enemy. Wash away anything
you have not authored for my life. Protect me from
the devil's schemes. Give me eyes to see myself, not on
the world's eyes, but in your eyes. Abba Father, may I
know deep in my heart that I am holy, created in your
own image and set apart for your purposes. Open my
eyes to see my true beauty, a beauty that reflects your
heart. Fill me with your Holy Spirit and bless me
all the days of my life. I asked all this in the
mighty name of Jesus Christ.
Amen!

"Behold I will do something new, Now, it will spring
forth; Will you not be aware of it? I will even make a
roadway in the wilderness, rivers in the desert."
Isaiah 43:19

When I read this Scripture, I lightened up. I was feeling sad and lonely because I did not have my children and grandchildren to celebrate my 75th birthday with. I know that God is doing "new things." Rayma Worship Center has not been bearing good fruit for 9 years since it was birthed. There have been a lot of roadblocks and road bumps along the way. But, thank God that He made me aware of all these things that are happening. I had several challenges, trials and tribulations, trying to break the bad habits that I saw things that is hindering the growth of Rayma Worship Center.

"Now it shall spring forth", God is doing transformations and changes for Rayma Worship Center for it to become a Holy Spirit-filled church. It shall spring up like grass in the spring, so green and beautiful and fresh; or it shall bud like the new growth from a tree branch or an opening flower bud- a beautiful figure denoting the manner in which the events of Divine Providence come to pass.

*"I will even make a way in the wilderness. "*The prophet describes the anxious care which God would show in protecting his people, and providing for them in conducting them to their native land.

I am praying for revival not only in Narvacan, but in Ilocos Region. But I need to focus on the people of my village (Abour) first. I know that God is making a way for us to get out of our situation. I thank God for His protection that the property was not taken away as the enemy planned. I thank God for the struggles that I knew was just temporary. I thank God for sending me Pastor Bong in the meantime, for he cannot commit to fulltime because of several responsibilities in his ministry.

God also promised *"streams in the wasteland"*. Rayma Worship Center is going to be revived exceedingly and abundantly. I know that the Great Revival is coming. The streams of new believers, and non-believers will be flowing into Rayma Worship Center. God is going to supply all our needs: a full-time pastor, a good shepherd who can lead his sheep, a self-contained bachelor apartment at the back of the sanctuary, an anointed worship team, and more salvation and baptisms.

My Prayer

I thank you God for opening my eyes today. Thank you that, you are doing new things. What is that new thing? Show me, Lord. Talk to me God! I believe you are working things out for me, and with pastor Bong in finding me a pastor for Rayma Worship Center. Yes, I agree we need a "new pastor". Let your will be done! Let your kingdom come! I pray Father God that you give me wisdom, knowledge and understanding on everything I do. I praise you! I glorify your name! I adore you! I commit and surrender my all to you in Jesus Name I pray.
Amen.

SECTION 35

Divine Connection

January 22, 2020

I was sitting at the front of Rayma Worship Center one morning while waiting for the materials to arrive for the making of the gate and driveway.

An elderly man was passing by the church and he stopped and asked me, *"What is this building for?"* Then I told him, *"It's Rayma Worship Center, a non-denominational building for worship, everyone is welcome"*. I introduced myself and he did the same. When I told him who my father was, he told me that he used to work for my father during the tobacco years.

He told me his name is Santiago. He is a Catholic in religion. He served in the church in town for many, many years, and he knows the Bible well. He is a very knowledgeable and curious man. He asked me to show him our Ilocano and English Bible. He was counting the numbers of book in both Bibles. He is trying to make comparison to Catholic Bible and other version of the Bible.

He asked me if he can have them and I gave them. He is interested to attend our Sunday service and told him that he is welcome. Everyone is welcome to Rayma Worship Center. I told him it's not religion that saves us, it's the relationship with Jesus that matters. He asked me if we could do Bible Study in his village, Dinaloaon. I agreed to do it on Saturdays at 2:00 pm. He said that he will invite his neighbors, who are all Catholic, which is great.

Then the following day, my workers told me when I stopped by the church that Santiago was searching for me to discuss some religious matter. While I was there, Santiago showed up and he was relieved. He was telling me about a religious group that he is involved with was having a conference and discussing certain issues. He just wants my opinions about them, so he can voice his opinion on the matter. He just needed clear clarification to express his opinion. He was very happy and appreciative about our meeting. I have respect for him and I also have respect for his belief.

Today, I see and I am believing: new generation, new vision, new program, new harvest, and new beginnings! Now I am more on fire for the Lord!

January 24, 2020

> *"Ask, and it will be given to you, seek and you will find, knock, and it will be opened to you."*
> *Matthew 7:7*

My prayer

Father God, you know my heart about Rayma Worship Center.

ASK:

- To find a committed full-time pastor for Rayma Worship Center; and

- To find a worship team and leader to lead worship that is also committed and anointed and passionate to serve the Lord.

SEEK:

- I am seeking for lost souls that want to be saved. May God lead me to them. I am seeking for spiritual growth and maturity for Rayma Worship Center. I am not looking for quantity, I am looking for quality Christians.

KNOCK:

- I keep knocking to God to open the door for more spiritual and physical strength, more harvest, more patience and more endurance and perseverance and provision.

Let the river of God flow in Rayma Worship Center

SECTION 36

Change of Location

FEB 2, 2020

"The Lord is my light and my salvation.
Whom shall I fear?
The Lord is the defense of my life. Whom shall I dread?
When evildoers came upon me to devour my flesh, my
adversaries and my enemies, they stumble and fell.
Though a host encamp against me,
my heart will not fear;
Though war arise against me, in spite
of this I shall be confident.
One thing I have asked from the Lord, that I shall seek:
That I may dwell in the house of the Lord
all the days of my life,
To behold the beauty of the Lord
And to meditate in His temple.

For in the day of trouble He will conceal me
in His tabernacle;
In the secret place of His tent, He will hide me;
He will offer in His tent sacrifices with shouts of joy;
I will sing yes; I will sing praises to the Lord.
Hear, O Lord, when I cry with my voice, and be gra-
cious to me and answer me.
Now as for me, I said in my prosperity,
"I will never be moved."
O Lord, by Your favor You have made my
mountain to stand strong;
You hid Your face, I was dismayed.
To You, O Lord, I called,
And to the Lord I made supplication:
'What profit is there in my blood, if I
go down to the pit?
Will the dust praise You? Will it declare
Your faithfulness?
Hear, O Lord, and be gracious to me;
O Lord be my helper.'
You have turned for me my mourning into dancing;
You have loosed my sackcloth and girded me
with gladness,
That my soul may sing praise to You and not be silent.
O Lord my God, I will give thanks to You forever."
Psalm 27

When we face serious illnesses, financial struggles,
dangerous situations, addictions, or some unexpected
problem, immediately, a spirit of fear will try to gain
stronghold or access in your mind. If you fail to take
authority over it, it will control and dominate your

heart and mind until you are no longer trusting and believing the Lord.

When God gives you a promise and directs you to take a step of faith and act on that promise, a wall of fear will try to block you. God has spoken, "Now is your time!" Now is your time to receive the fulfillment of the promise of God has given you---to take a hold of God's promises, that wall of fear must be demolished.

When God directs you to step out in faith on His Word to witness, pray for the sick, or launch out into any area of ministry, a spirit of fear will come against your mind to hinder you from doing the will of God.

I am overwhelmed with what is going around me.

Fear has gripped me. These Scripture readings gave me the confidence that God is faithful that God is my helper and God is gracious to me. God is telling me that He will turn my mourning into dancing. I will continue to seek Him, meditate on His Word, and Praise Him and thank Him for everything He has done for me.

I recognized that this fear is not from God. It is from the enemy, to try and hinder me from the fulfillment of what God has commanded me to do. The enemy tried everything but I know that God is with me always. My faith doesn't allow me to stop after the blessings even though there were hurdles to overcome. I was willing to go forward and get the power that God has promised me to fulfill my purpose in life.

My Prayer

Lord Jesus, thank you for helping me recognize fear for what it is- a sin. It immobilizes my faith and hinders me from possessing God's promises. It causes me to

disobey God, and/or prevents me from doing the works
of God and operating in the Gifts of the Spirit. I reject
fear in my life in Jesus Name! Amen

I travelled to La Union to attend the funeral of my cousin with Reye's Syndrome. I stayed and visited my two cousins Linda and Carrie, who are also visiting from Seattle. We also went to Baguio City to tour different places.

La Union, officially the Province of La Union, is a province in the Philippines located in the Ilocos Region in the Island of Luzon. Its capital is the City of San Fernando, which also serves as the regional center of the Ilocos Region.

La Union is also known as the Garden Coast because of its Botanical Garden that showcases—a Fernery, Palmary, Fragrance Garden, Sunken Garden, Evergreen Garden, and Arid Paradise, and Shade Garden—with flora and fauna that are homegrown only in the Philippines

Meanwhile, Baguio is best known as the "Summer Capital of the Philippines", with its cool climate making this a spot to escape the chaotic scenes in Manila. The city is also home to tropical pine forests, lending the city the nickname "City of Pines". Baguio is a mountain town of universities and resorts.

While in La Union, I developed persistent cough again so I went to the hospital for checkup. I had X-ray and found out I have pneumonia again. Antibiotic was prescribed, and after, I felt better.

During my stay in La Union, I went to San Fernando Christian Community Church. It is a non-denominational, Bible-believing church. I met the Senior Pastor Tim, who is a non-Filipino and married to Filipina lady who started that church 30 years ago. I introduced myself as a missionary and asked for help to look for a full-time pastor also. The church' has many portables made of Sea containers converted into classrooms. Now he is in a process of building a brand-new Sanctuary, with a huge and beautiful design.

February 8, 2020

I went to visit my daughter Rowena's friend, Nette, in Dasmarinas. I took Partas bus, an air-conditioned bus from La Union to Manila, with Linda who is also on her way to the Airport. Nette and her husband picked me up at 4:00 am at the Airport and took me to their gorgeous house. I stayed with them for nine days while I was waiting for Lily, a missionary from Canada, to come back.

February 10, 2020

I went out with Nette and had lunch at Bahai Restaurant. In the evening, they asked me to join their regular family day at Modern Shanghai, with their two daughters, and their son. I also met Pastor Anthony briefly with his family. Pastor Anthony is the founder, CEO of Church of God (COG) in Dasmariñes, Philippines.

February 11, 2020

I joined their C2S Bible study group led by her husband, Noli. C2S means Connect 2 Souls. It was such an amazing Bible Study. I bought copies of their study manual and wanted to facilitate a Bible Study group in my community or at Rayma Worship Center. Their whole family was very much involved and active in their church, Church of God. Their children were all going to school and were also involved in worship teams, missions and many more activities in church. Their household is a very active and busy household, but a very happy and blessed family. You feel the love in them.

February 12, 2020

Nette and I went to Dawnwatch at Church of God at 5:00 am, which consisted of worship, teaching the verse *2 Timothy 6*, and prayer. Dawnwatch is a service to worship and pray to God before sunrise. It's such a refreshing way to attend the service and seeking God first before sunrise. The sacrifice to get up early morning to have a meeting with the Lord was amazing. It's a new way and good way to renew your mind before your busy day starts.

Honestly, these couple had a business of their own but they have so much time for God as well; leading, teaching and doing the work for God. They are blessed! I am privileged and honored to know them. I learned a lot from them, balancing their time with family, business, personal and time with God. They have a balanced life.

At 5-6:30 pm, Nette booked a tour for me to the facility of COG in Dasmarinas. Awesome facilities! Great people!

At 7-8:30 pm, we attended a midweek service. Awesome worship! Great message! I got filled and I can't stop, I wanted more! I was enjoying every moment of my time for change.

February 13, 2020

We went to Dawnwatch at 5:00 am. After, we went shopping for pots and pans for Rayma Worship Center's supply. We had lunch at Savory Chicken at the Mall. Nette went to work that afternoon, and I got a chance to minister to Tessie, Nette's helper, while she was giving me a back massage. She got saved that day and I gave her a Bible. I am still in touch with her and she is reading her Bible. Praise God!

February 14, Hearts Day!

We went to Dawnwatch at 5:00 am again, and I met Vicky, one of Rowena's acquaintances. Nette invited her to come back home with us at her house. We had a good fellowship and coffee.

Nette knew my heart; that I was looking for a pastor for Rayma Worship Center.

At 10:30 am, Nette wanted me to meet Pastor Anthony in person to see if he could help. She managed to get an appointment to meet with him because he has a very busy schedule. His gorgeous office is on the fifth floor of the Church building, overlooking a panoramic view of the city, in three corners of his office. Great man of God! He connected me with the Regional Pastor for Northern Luzon Region.

Then, we attended an Excel service. Amazing!

February 16, 2020

I pretty well stayed in church all day that day. I did not want to leave in case I missed something. I was talking to a group of volunteers who were preparing to go to streets in groups. Each group was given certain areas to go evangelize. Today, I attended three services back-to-back. The worship was amazing and powerful. Amazing experience!

I met a lady who operates 100 Lost sheep Ministry in Paliparan. She invited me to go visit her place and meet the single mothers and children. She made a schedule on when to visit.

February 17, 2020

Today, I decided to stay home. I did not feel good. Her housekeeper took me for a walk around Mini- Jerusalem, that's what I call it. The names of the street were Succoth, Jerusalem, Bethlehem, Bethel, Bethesda, Jericho, Ephesus, Emmaus. I was fascinated by the street names. It reminds me of the Israel trip me and my husband took with Bethel Gospel Tabernacle group in Jerusalem, where I got baptized at the Jordan River.

February 18, 2020

Nette took me to 100 Lost Sheep Ministry location. This lady and her husband support single mom and their children. These women and their children lived in a squatter area, where hunger is imminent and lots of needs are required. I prayed with mothers that are unsaved. There were lots of children and babies to be fed. She was asking me to do a feeding program. This is another feeding project that needs to be addressed in the near future, God-willing.

February 19, 2020

Nette and Noli drove me to the airport to meet Lily, who is arriving from Canada. I am so blessed to have met Nette and Noli. They helped me so much and they gave me a place to stay and took me to places where I could not have gone on my own. Their life is great because I believe that God has blessed them because they are willing to serve and obey God. God showed me the difference of success when you are serving God and the poverty in the village when you resist to obey and want to know God. This was an eye opener for me and this taught me a lesson that sacrifice and obedience is the key to success.

Lily's flight arrived safely. We took a taxi to Partas bus station bound to Ilocos Sur. The taxi driver who drove us is a Christian. I shared with him about the Church of God in Dasmarinas.

Pastor Bong was already waiting at the bus terminal, as he was also returning to Ilocos Sur, so we took the same Partas bus.

Upon arrival in Narvacan where the municipality of my village is located, we took a tricycle to take us to Rayma Worship Center. We went directly to the church building, where we will be staying from now on. The bachelor's apartment was complete and I got everything we needed. Praise God! We slept at the church apartment for the first time. It was good!

I was starting to see a light with regards to finding a pastor. I was hopeful and believed that the door that was opened was a door of possibility. God provided me a place to stay, and he led me to connect with good and loving Christian family.

The story of Pastor Anthony is very inspiring. In 2000, The Lord envisioned Himself to Pastor Anthony in a dream saying, *"I will bless you."*

He imparted this gift to the church which initiated the plan to start building the church's own sanctuary. To fulfill this, the church had to move to Marilag Subdivision along Aguinaldo Highway before December 2002 to avoid renewing contract with the UMC warehouse for another five years. As God's favor was truly upon the church, it was able to move to Marilag in time. It was also in 2002 when the church became Church of God Dasmarinas, World Missions of the Philippines with 1,500 members.

In 2006, the church sanctuary was completely finished and continued to become a witness to numerous ministries. Then 2008, the COG Jabez was built through the collected funds from a concert.

Then came the annual Prayer &Fasting during year 2010, where Pastor Anthony saw a vision. In the vision, he saw the Lord Jesus Christ approached him at the back of the COG Jabez sanctuary where the fasting was held. At that moment, he fell on his knees in awe of His presence. Suddenly, he turned into a jar. Then he began seeing the scene between the Lord and himself as a jar. Then the Lord put His heavenly money into the jar. Pastor Anthony said and claimed, *"For the church!"* Then afterwards, he woke up from a trance. After the vision, Pastor Anthony heeded the call of the Lord to build the Generation Blessing Building, also known as the GenBless Building, a five-story building that will accommodate the increasing population of the church and to provide the needs of its members.

Today the Lord has continued to bless and enlarge the church, with almost 15,000 strong members and 3,700 dedicated workers ready to fulfill the vision of turning Dasmarinas into a born-again city, and eventually turning our country into Born-Again Pilipinas.

COG have eight services every Sunday. The church holds about 2,000 people per service, excluding overflow.

SECTION 37

God Is At Work

Feb 20-25, 2020

I was very busy meeting pastors from different churches around the area connected with COG organization. I also met with the regional representative and discussed the options and their policy. Then, as I took consideration on the pros and cons, I decided not to go that route. And I also prayed about it and that's not where God intended me to do.

So, now we are back to the drawing board. I know I still have Pastor Bong doing some searching. He has given me a slight indication that he was almost there, so I had a little hope. Time was running out and I only had a couple of weeks left before I leave for Canada. I had faith that I will find someone right for Rayma Worship Center. Pastor Bong reassured me that he will find someone, and I believed him.

What I found interesting was that every one of them had an agenda and motive. They didn't consider the moral value of why this church was built in the first place. Rayma Worship Center was built in faith with the purpose of finding and saving lost souls, and not to compete or to make it as a business. Joining an organization was not a part of God's plan. It is a legacy to recognize Rayma as a child of God who wants to have abundant harvest of souls. As a family, we need to carry that legacy where our family, their children, and their children's children will carry from generation to generation. I don't feel it's right for an organization to take over and lose the value of its creation.

SECTION 38

Confusion

March, 2020

Lily was booked to go back to Canada on March 20, 2020 and I was booked to depart on March 30, 2020.

Covid 19 was in the air all over the world. I was almost done with my mission here except for one important thing, finding a full-time pastor. I had about three weeks left.

I was so confused on what to do. Do I go back to Canada with Lily or stay till the end of March as originally booked?

My friend from Malaysia invited me to go visit her. My son and daughter told me to stay put. It's Covid! What I did not realize was how serious this Covid was. I did not think too much of anything, because we did not listen to the news over there. At first, they were just requiring masks, can't have two passengers in a motorbike, and less capacity on public transportation. I think I was not very concerned or paid too much attention with what was going on.

My daughter was calling me to come back home with Lily, and I finally agreed, so she managed to change my flight.

March 1, 2020

Rayma Worship Center was serviced by COG pastor with their sound system, worship team and some members of their congregation. There were 30-40 people in attendance. It was a powerful service. Pastor Bong was not present. I feel there was a conflict between the two organizations.

I started inviting friends and relatives to have dinner and fellowship with them. It was my down time to enjoy and smell the roses; what God had done. We were invited to speak to few different churches. More tensions are building up between people around me. I think at this point, I was losing patience and was feeling homesick and tired.

But, even on my tiredness and discouragement, God still sent me people that needed salvation even when I was not searching. Just sitting outside, reading and journaling, three young ladies stopped by selling pens. One lady asked what this building is for, and I explained and told her, "It's a worship center where people come and fellowship. Its non –denominational and everyone is welcome." She asked, *'How do I get saved?'* I replied, "It's simple". I just want to ask you few questions if you are okay with that." She said, *"I'm okay with it."* I asked, ", she replied yes. *"Do you believe that Jesus died and bled to cleanse you from your sin?"* she replied, "yes". *"Do you believe that the third day He rose from the dead?"* She replied "yes." *"Do you believe that He lived?"* She replied, "yes". I asked her to join me in praying the sinner's prayer, asking God for forgiveness of her sin, and accepting Jesus as her personal Savior. She was very happy, I gave her a Bible and told her to find and join a Christian church where she lived. The other one is already a Christian and the other one was not interested. One soul made a difference. Praise God!

More drama! Never mind, not mission related. I need to leave the village for a bit. Marcello and Tessie invited us to go to visit their daughter and family in Suyo, so Lily and I went with them.

March 11, 2020
Suyo is a fourth-class Municipality composed of eight Barangays and forty-five Sitios.

The vase mountainous areas are planted with bananas, camote (sweet potato), bamboo and bolo, mango, ipil-ipil, ginger, rambutan, coffee, pineapple, cacao, and tiger grass which is the material used for broom making. The industry that is prevailing in the province of Ilocos Sur is "basi (wine)making" and vinegar making, and broom making.

While in Suyo with Tessie and Marcelo, we met pastor Rodel, Sherry's lovely family, Pastor Dennis and family, and Pastor Amy. They all gave us a warm welcome and they arranged a special service the day after we arrived and they asked me to give a message and Lily to give her testimony. People there were very appreciative.

I thanked the Lord for the day. It was such a joy to be with family and friends enjoying each other and God's beautiful creation. Beautiful mountains, streams, hills, valleys, trees of all kind, people of all ages, and faith of all kind. We are all created in God's image. Seeing the love for each other no matter who they are is an amazing trait. I can feel the love around people. It is such a different atmosphere when you are surrounded with believers.

In my hometown, there was so much anger, bitterness, jealousy and hatred in their hearts. I hope and pray that one day the people in my hometown will be touched, they would repent and that they surrender their lives to Jesus. This is my fervent prayer, in Jesus' Name! It reminds me of what Jesus went through His hometown in Capernaum. He said, *"A prophet has no respect in His own hometown."* I experienced what is like to be unwanted.

March 7, 2020

We had a trip to Sarmingan COG service. Sarmingan is a Barangay of Narvacan, Ilocos Sur Philippines

Ilocos Sur Province is a part of Luzon region. Ilocos Sur comprises of 32 municipalities.

Narvacan is a 2nd class municipality in the province of Ilocos Sur. Narvacan is 375 kms from metro Manila and 32 kms from Vigan. Narvacan has 34 Barangays. Abuor is one, where Rayma Worship Center is situated.

Narvacan was discovered by a Spanish expeditionary force sent from Vigan by the military officer and navigator, Captain Juan de Salcedo in 1576. The Spanish expeditionary forces were shipwrecked along the town coast, when they were being rescued by the natives. The Spaniards asked the natives what was the name of their place. The native resident leader replied in "Ilocano dialect", by asking the Spaniard, "Nalbakan" (meaning are you shipwrecked?). The Spaniards thought this is the answer to his question and from then on, the place was referred to as Narvacan.

DEMOGRAPHIC

Narvacan residents are largely Roman Catholic. A sizable minority of Iglesia ni Christo, Methodist, Christians and Jehovah's Witnesses are present.

ECONOMY

Narvacan is located in a valley of the Island of Luzon, surrounded by mountains, a fertile region with cool tropical climate. The principal crops are corn, cotton, indigo, rice, sugarcane and tobacco.

SCRIPTURE READING

*"And He also went on to say to the one who had
invited Him, 'When you give a luncheon or a dinner,*

do not invite your friends or your brothers or your relatives or rich neighbors, otherwise they may also invite you in return and that will be your repayment.'

'But you give a reception, invite the poor, the crippled, the lame, the blind, and you will be blessed, since they do not have the means to repay you; for you will be repaid at the resurrection of the righteous.' When one of those who were reclining at the table with Him heard this, he said to Him, 'Blessed is everyone who will eat bread in the kingdom of God!' But He said to him, 'A man was giving a big dinner, and he invited many; and at the dinner hour he sent his slave to say to those who had been invited, 'Come; for everything is ready now.' But they all alike began to make excuses. The first one said to him, 'I have bought a piece of land and I need to go out and look at it; please consider me excused.' Another one said, 'I have bought five yokes of oxen, and I am going to try them out; please consider me excused.' Another one said, 'I have married a wife, and for that reason I cannot come.' And the slave came back and reported this to his master. Then the head of the household became angry and said to his slave, 'Go out at once into the streets and lanes of the city and bring in here the poor and crippled and blind and lame.' And the slave said 'Master, you commanded has been done, and still there is room.' And the master said to the slave, 'Go out into the highways and along the hedges, and compel them to come in, so that my house will be filled. For I tell you, none of those men who are invited shall taste the dinner.'"

Luke 14:12-23

In this passage, I observed that if you invite your relatives, friends, rich people, neighbors and town mates to come, every one of them have excuses especially if they don't want you to succeed. As a host, the king has prepared a great banquet for his people but his people let him down by making lame excuses not to attend. His people want to embarrass the king.

But instead, he asked his servant to go to the streets, allies, roads, highways, hedges to invite less fortunate people. Lame, crippled, blind, poor, the needy to come fill the place and eat the good food he prepared for his well.

When a dinner guest said "Blessed is he who will feast in the Kingdom of God," Jesus responded with the parable of the great dinner, suggesting that the chosen people had declined the invitation because of other priorities and that Gentiles would take their place. The chosen people were not willing to give the master the priority that he deserved.

Discipleship is costly. Jesus teaches them that discipleship carries a high price tag. Those who aspire to follow him need to count the cost before signing on the dotted line. Jesus demands commitment, an unpopular word these days. Jesus does not make discipleship easy. He does not offer an easy payment plan. He never disguises the cost of discipleship. Instead, he writes the price tag large for all to see.

My Prayer

Lord Jesus, Heavenly Father, I need help to harvest souls. This is what this church, Rayma Worship Center, I believe is for. I asked that you revive this town and this church in Jesus Name.

SECTION 39

Be a Servant

"For you, brethren, became imitators of the churches
of God in Christ Jesus that are in Judea, for you also
endured the same sufferings at the hands of your own
countrymen, even as they did from the Jews."
1 Thessalonians 2:14

As a servant of God, I also endured the same sufferings at the hand of my own countrymen; rejection, persecution and betrayal and insult.

"But after we had already suffered and been
mistreated in Philippi, as you know, we had the
boldness in our God to speak to you the gospel
of God amid much opposition."
1 Thessalonians 2:2

I am ready to suffer. Paul was beaten, imprisoned in Philippi. Paul was hindered by imprisonment and death; threats from preaching the Gospel.

God gives us the strength to do His will. Boldness inspired by the Holy Spirit that is in us.

Be willing and ready to suffer, throw away impure motives.

"For our exhortation does not come from error or
impurity or by way of deceit."
1 Thessalonian 2:3

Paul did not seek money, home and popularity through sharing the Gospel.

This demonstration of persecution did not keep him and his team from doing the work of his kingdom.

God and his team did everything by God's approval.

Believers must do the work out of love and others.

DO NOT BE PLEASURE OF MAN

"But just as we have been approved by God to be
entrusted with the Gospel, so we speak, not as pleasing
men, but God who examines your hearts."
1 Thessalonians 2:4

Servanthood is not a matter of pleasing man but pleasing of God.

Servants are also tempted to alter the message they received from the Lord in order to become great.

The Gospel must never compromise though we can change the methods.

DO NOT BE GREEDY

*"For we never came with flattering speech, as you
know, nor with a pretext for greed—God is witness."*
1 Thessalonians 2:5

Paul proclaimed the truth with honesty. He was straight forward in word and actions. Paul did not preach what the people wanted to hear just to get the profit from them.

Beware of sugared gospel.

DO NOT SEEK PRAISE FOR MEN

*"Nor did we seek glory from men, either from you or
from others, even thou as apostles of Christ we might
have asserted our authority."*

Paul completely focused his efforts into presenting the gospel to the Thessalonians.

The Thessalonians changed because of the message.

We should witness for Christ and not for the impression we might make.

Servanthood is one of the ways we can be great in the kingdom of God. To become a servant of God, attitudes and values are required.

We should try to follow Paul's example. He was a sinful man. He did terrible things; he was a murderer. No matter what our past is, God is a forgiving God. He already redeemed us through the cross, died, paid for our sin, bled to cleanse and purify us and the third day He rose from the dead. Because He lived, so we also live.

*"I am crucified with Christ, nevertheless, I live…and
the life where now I live. I live by the faith of the Son of
God, who loved me and gave Himself for me."*
Galatians 2:20

March 8, 2020

Pastor Bong's Message:

What is God's purpose for your life?
Do you choose to be a victim or a victor?
You must walk in the highway of truth.

*"Jesus said, 'I am the way, the truth and the life. No
one comes to The Father except through me.'"*
John 14: 6

This is the message sign above the Rayma Worship Center front door.

SECTION 40

Benefits of Hearing and Reading the Word of God

Revelation 1:3

1. Reading and hearing the Word is a Blessing

> *"Blessed is the one who reads aloud the Words of this prophecy, and blessed are those who hear it and take heart what is written in it, because the time is near."*

2. Obedience is the key for more blessings

> *"If you obey the Lord your God and carefully follow all his commands I give you today, the Lord your God will set you high above all the nations on earth. All these blessings will come on you and accompany you if you obey the Lord your God: You will be blessed in the city and blessed in the country."*
> *Deuteronomy 28: 1-3*

3. What produces my decision making?

> *"So, then faith cometh by hearing, and hearing*
> *by the Word of God."*
> *Romans 10:17*

That is why it is so important that the Word comes first thing in the morning daily and consistently. He always directs your path in every decision you make in your daily life. Reading the Word and applying and doing what God commanded me to do is where I got the victory.

His Word encourages me when I am down. His Word lifts me up. His Word is true. His Word is alive.

4. What is God's purpose for your life?

God wants to bless you.

> *"In the beginning was the Word, and the Word was*
> *with God, and the Word was God."*
> *John 1:1*

Become Son of the living God. Purpose to know Him deeper and have an encounter with God; to get to know Him is by reading His Word. Don't be afraid.

SECTION 41

Desire to Have a Victorious Mind

"The Jews answered him, 'We have a law, and by that law He ought to die because He made Himself out to be the Son of God.' Therefore, when Pilate heard this statement, he was even more afraid; and he entered into the Praetorium again, and said to Jesus, 'Where are you from?' But Jesus gave Him no answer. So, Pilate said to Him, 'You do not speak to me? Do you not know that I have authority to release You, and I have the authority to crucify you?' Jesus answered, 'You would have no authority over Me, unless it had been given you from above; for this reason, he who delivered Me to you has the greater sin.'"
John 19: 7-11

Jesus paid the prize so we can have power to make a one hundred percent victorious mind. Satan no longer has power over us. He does not have power to make us sin. He cannot control our minds, thoughts, wills, and emotions. He has no power over us except what we allow him to have. Yet, eighty nine percent of Christians today are living in defeat because they do not recognize that their minds are Satan's battlefield, or they fail to resist and take offensive action against him.

There are Christians who are being tempted with carnal desires and lusts of the flesh. A fierce battle is raging within them. Satan has a vice-like grip on their minds and they are unable to be free of his tormenting spirits. They are unable to resist temptation and are yielding to themselves a result, their minds are filled with fear, guilt and condemnation and they are defeated.

The majority of Christians today, are in a weakened state of minds, and are victims of depression. They are gripped with a sense of hopelessness, frustration and despair. They are spiritually immobilized, unable to release their faith to think clearly, to cope with the problems and circumstances they are facing. In these depressed state-of-minds, they feel the only way out is to escape, to run from the problems. In some severe cases of depression their minds are in such a turmoil, that they begin to think about suicide.

There are Christians sitting in our pews today who are oppressed by Satan. They are tormented, frustrated and confused. Yet they are unable to take authority over Satan's forces and walk in Christ victory because they do not know where and how Satan is attacking.

There is no reason why God's people today should live in defeat. There is no reason why they should be confused, worried, fearful, anxious, depressed, or oppressed in their minds. Jesus did not pay the supreme price and gave His life as a sacrifice to free us from the power of sin so that we would live in victory over the enemy fifty percent, seventy percent or even ninety five percent of the time.

He did not give us the power of the Holy Spirit so we would be overcome by the enemy and walk around discouraged and defeated in our minds. Jesus came to earth to destroy the works of the devil and free us from Satan's power so that we would not be fearful, weak, and powerless. Jesus paid the price so that you and I have one hundred percent victorious mind one hundred percent of the time.

I decree and declare that: "Satan has no power over me except what I permit or allow him to have. Therefore, I will not allow him to have any power at all."

SECTION 42

More Problems and Trials

March 9 2020

*"Then it happened when David and his men came to
Ziklag on the third day, the Amelekites had made a
raid on the Negev and on Ziklag, and had overthrown
Ziklag and burned it with fire; and they took captives
the women and all who were in it, both small and
great, without killing anyone, and carried them off
and went their way. When David and his men came
to the city, behold, it was burned with fire, and their
wives and their sons and their daughters had been
taken captive. Then David and the people who were
with him lifted their voices and wept until there was
no strength in them to weep. Now David's two wives
had been taken captive, Ahinoam and Jesreelites and
Abigail the widow of Nabal the Carmelite."*
1 Samuel 30:1-6

Moreover, David was greatly distressed because the people spoke of stoning him, for all the people were embittered because of his sons and his daughters, but David strengthened himself in the Lord his God.

David was distressed on what happened to his place, to his wives, and his sons and daughters. Plus, they planned to stone him. It is human nature to react and get distressed when these things happen to our family and when we faced trials and circumstances such as grave as what David has experienced. David and all his belongings have been destroyed and his wives' sons and daughters were taken captive. How awful and tragic it is if it happened to us? How would we react?

So, what David did was he prayed, he wept aloud until he did not have strength to do it anymore. And God gave him strength on his weakness.

And it was the same that God did for me after praying, seeking, and knocking. God can do it for you also. He is our strength when we are weak.

This again reminded me of all the things that happened to me in the beginning of our Mission. Rayma Worship Center was abandoned and all the members, with the pastor that was in-charge then, left without notice or discussions of any problem.

The pre- arranged accommodations, prior to departure was changed five times because of misleading information and promises not fulfilled.

There were a lot of uncertainties that arisen. I just had to keep seeking God for guidance and He did get me out of trouble. He provided my every need at all times. He did not leave me nor forsake me because He is always walking with me.

The place in my hometown where I was supposed to stay changed their mind and so I had no place to stay. Another family did not want me to stay at their place even though they have a room.

Thank God I had another family that was willing to let me stay in their daughter's house which was empty. I had someone watching me all the time, making food for me, supply me with water, etc. and she stayed with me at night. Loling and her whole family helped me a lot. I thank God for their love, compassion and their kindness. They are a humble family. Loling is the dedicated caretaker of Rayma Worship Center. God Bless her and her family.

Then I decided to make a bachelor's apartment behind the church sanctuary. Lots of empty space and a bathroom are already there. All I have to do is buy a stove, bed mattress, pots and pans, rice cooker, and few utensils and it worked. I had peace, praise the Lord. Lily and I lived here when she came back again from Canada.

I thank God for giving me the wisdom, the provision and guidance throughout my journey. I thank God for giving me the strength to carry on with all the drama and challenges of mission. Thank God that He helped me face all the disappointments, discouragements, and gave me strength to not quit and allow the enemy to win over me.

The fact remained that I still do not have a full-time pastor for Rayma Worship Center. There was only a week left at this point. What are the chances of finding one? Lord God, I need a Miracle!

Pastor Bong has been preaching during Sundays since December 15, 2019. He is a faithful servant of the Lord!

My Prayer

Dear Heavenly Father,

I thank you for all that you have done. Throughout the mission trip from November 6, 2019 to now, you have been with me all the time. Thank you that you did not leave me or forsake me in times of trouble and you gave me strength when I am weak. I thank you for everything you did during this mission.

My most urgent prayer, Father God, is to revive
Rayma Worship Center and your people in my
hometown. This is your house, your temple, not
mine. Please God continue to increase, grow your
church in Jesus' Name! Bring people in so they
can see your goodness. Bless your people Lord in
Jesus name!

*"Do not cast me off in the time of old age; Do not
forsake me when my strength fails."*
Psalm 71:9

I am now 75 years old, with gray hair and frail eyes, but I am
strong in the Lord. He gave me strength. I walk around with a
cane, I rode in a jeepney, tricycle, and motorbike rides if necessary.
I am not afraid to do the work of God. I am safe and secure in
His hands.

SECTION 43

Miracles and Answered Prayers

March 10, 2020
Covid-19 Pandemic is announced.

President Duterte of the Philippines announced the closure of commercial passengers and international flights as of March 19 at 11:.59 pm.

March 15, 2020
My Last Sunday Service at Rayma Worship Center.

This was my last Sunday service before going back to Canada. Pastor Bong came with his wife, Amelia, to do the service. He told me that a pastor is coming today to meet me. I was shocked and thankful to God that He never let me down. He came and attended the service, then we met. His name is Pastor Exodo. He will be an assistant pastor to pastor Bong. I was so ecstatic and I thank God for another miracle He gave me!

Thank you, Jesus!

MIRACLE #1
March 16, 2020
THE QUESTION WAS, ARE WE GOING HOME?

Now this is serious and very concerning because our flight was scheduled on March 20, 2020 at 8:00 pm. So, Lily, myself, and my daughter Rowena were panicking that we cannot go home to Canada as scheduled. It seems so impossible at this point. If worst comes to worse, we will stay longer. But God did not stop us from hoping for miracle. Lily and Rowena were constantly checking on the update of the flight situation. I called my Sanggunian friend to help me inquire on what is happening about the flight cancellation and commercial buses. She searched and inquired for me. She recommended us to get a medical certificate clearance. She arranged for a nurse and assistance to do a medical clearance in my hometown just to be prepared in case it changes. So, we got our medical clearance certificate. I was telling the nurse that we might not be able to fly back because of the restrictions and cancellation of international flights on March 19, 2020 at 11:59 pm.

Then, she mentioned that she just gave a medical certificate to a couple from Edmonton, Canada. Their flight is on March 20 at 3:00 pm. She gave me the contact number of the couple to confirm details and they said that their flight is not cancelled. Also, when Lily checked our flight status, it's not cancelled. So, we started packing and preparing.

Then, the next problem was finding a private car to take us to Manila Airport since there were no commercial busses or transportation running. The protocol at that time was: once the driver enters Manila, they have to be quarantined in Manila for two weeks, so it was very difficult to find somebody to drive us to the airport. Then again, I called my Sanggunian friend and asked for help. She gave me a list of documents we needed to photocopy and she will try to find us a driver to take us to Manila Airport. We got all the documents photocopied; passports, air tickets, and medical certificates. I thank God that she was able to find somebody who is willing to take a risk for us to go to Manila Airport.

MIRACLE#2

Then we took off to Manila Airport thinking that it will take us 10 hours to reach there. It took us only five and a half hours, without toll. It was a straight drive through except for a few check points to check our temperature and check our documents.

MIRACLE#3

Then, we reached the Airport way ahead of time. The airport is only open to passengers who are boarding two hours before their flight schedule. So, people are all sitting and standing outside the airport entrance. The place was packed. We decided to go and check into a hotel. There was no Hotel available near the Airport. We found a hotel that charged per hour. I have never seen or heard of it before, and yes, you read it correctly... hourly rate! We did not have any choice, we booked ourselves for 12 hours and had a good sleep and shower.

When we checked out, the receptionist told us there are only few drivers that are available and willing to drive and we took the risk. So, we had to wait a long time to find somebody, and we did.

MIRACLE#4

Then, we got to Manila Airport and checked in without any problem, Thank God!

We boarded the plane. It was a very pleasant and uneventful flight, and again, I Thank God!

This was the biggest miracle: that we did not get stuck in the Philippines during Covid-19 Pandemic.

MIRACLE #5

These experiences of miracles happen when you are obedient and trust God that He is in control. I have learned to lean on God and not trust my own understanding. God makes a way where there seems to be no way!

I arrived home safely, but again; I developed another cough. I went to the hospital to have it checked. They did the usual X-ray and blood test. Again, it was pneumonia. I was given another prescription of Antibiotics and thank God I got better. I was also tested for Covid and it was negative.

May 2020

I got this shocking news that Pastor Bong died while he was preaching. He collapsed and never woke up. It was a big tragedy to lose a good man of God. I am so grateful for all the help and support for Rayma Worship Center and finding us a Pastor. I believed it's all God's plan. "All things work together for good."

The rest of 2021, Rayma Worship Center was active with Sunday services, weekly prayer meeting, baptisms, and worship practice.

On December, I had arranged for an Engineer to put an addition to the existing building and get an estimate what it will cost. The cost was outrageous. Then, I again started seeking and asking God what to do. What is His will. Let His will be done.

YEAR 2022

I believed that 2022 was the year for Rayma Worship Center. I did Daniel's fasting and praying for 21 days; no meat, no sugar, and no bread. I was fasting and praying for the construction of The New Sanctuary (Lord's House) and Mission House (God's Servants

House). I started from January 9 to January 30. I felt very good and lost a few pounds.

February 3, 2022

Again, I contacted my Sanggunian friend to find out if she knew an Engineer to construct a Sanctuary and Mission House. She said yes, the Engineer who built her daughters house and does a lot of work in the Municipality where she works. Then, she was sending me different plans, style, and options. We finally agreed on one plan, and she got me the estimate to do the construction from start to finish. It will take about four to five months to complete. We agreed on the prize and the payment plan.

The groundbreaking took place on February 15, 2022. It took eighteen years to complete and fulfill my vision. It's worth every minute, every struggle, every road block, every betrayal, every disappointment, every pain, every sickness, and everything that I experienced during my journey.

I hope that everyone reading this book will find your dream, vision, and your God-given gift for your life. I hope and pray that you learned something and made an impact in your life; that God will reveal His purpose and plan for your life; that you will obey and follow God's command all the way until it's done. It does not matter how long it takes, God will help you and lead you all the way. There is nothing impossible with God. It is not easy but at the end God will reward you and God will say, "well done my faithful servant."

Many Blessing to all the readers!

"May we so live that day when the Lord may say to us,
'Well done, thou good and faithful servant; thou hast
been faithful over few things. I will make thee ruler
over many things: enter thou into the joy of the Lord.'"
Matthew 25:21

VISION FULFILLED.
MISSION ACCOMPLISHED.
HALLELUJAH!

The Rayma Worship Center has been in the wilderness for 9 years; not bearing good fruit and had no reliable shepherd to watch the sheep, no transparency, accountability, and no structure. Jesus promised *"He will make a way in the wilderness and rivers in the desert."*

Printed in Canada